The Cruise of the Fairweather

The Cruise of the Fairweather

Suttie Adams

Slack Water Press
Los Gatos, California

Slack Water Press, Los Gatos 95032
www.slackwaterpress.com

Copyright © 2012 Jon Adams
All rights reserved

ISBN 978-0-9797613-5-5

Cover design: warzecha, formgeberei

Cover image: Photograph, Suttie Adams, Schooner *Fairweather*, 1960

A Green Book
The paper used in this publication meets the standards for sustainable forestry.

For Rick, the Navigator

Contents

Illustrations	ix
Preface	xiii
Introduction	xvii
West Coast	1
South Seas	33
East Indies	67
Indian Ocean	105
Mediterranean	131
Atlantic Ocean	163
Afterword	179

Illustrations

Suttie and Fairweather	xii
Sausalito Boat Yard	xvi
The Sails	xx
Getting Underway	xxiv
Rick	10
Puerto Vallarta	18
Yalapa Anchorage	20
Yalapa Waterfall	22
Sailing West	32
School at Sea	36
Bill	40
Manihi Atoll	44
Papeete	48
Bora Bora	52
Samoa	56
Becalmed	66
Auckland	68
Asleep on Deck	70
Nouméa	78
The Chart Table	86

The Outrigger	90
From the Bowsprit	94
Baggywrinkle	104
Repairs	106
Great Nicobar	110
Cruising	114
Savo Royal National Park	118
Mandraki Harbor	130
Beirut	134
Mel and Tiare	142
Bonifacio	150
Ajaccio	152
San Tropez	156
The Topsail	162
Fishing	166
Valerie Queen	168
Suttie and Rick	172
The Golden Gate	178

Suttie and Fairweather

Preface

This book is an account of the schooner *Fairweather's* circumnavigation, San Francisco to San Francisco, a world cruise that began by sailing down the west coast of Mexico, and then by sailing west: across the South Seas, the East Indies, the Indian Ocean, the Mediterranean Sea, and the Atlantic Ocean, and then back up the west coast of Mexico. The cruise lasted four years, from March 1961 to April 1965. This account is based on the journal that Suttie Adams kept during the cruise, supplemented at times with details from *Fairweather's* logbook, which Suttie also kept. During the four years of the cruise, the *Fairweather* sailed 35,566 miles, spent 349 days at sea, and visited 103 ports. Was it a successful cruise? Well, many of the original crew were still aboard when *Fairweather* sailed back under the Golden Gate and into San Francisco Bay. Those few who left the schooner during the cruise never left willingly, with the possible exception of Bill Adams, the original captain, but let Suttie tell that story.

It has been forty-eight years since the world cruise of the *Fairweather* ended in San Francisco. During that time I inherited both my mother's journal and *Fairweather's* logbook, and a few years ago I used them extensively to write *The Cruise of the Jest*, a fictional version of that long ago world cruise. I wrote the fictional version because I wanted to tell what it was like, or as Conrad put it, "to make you hear, to make you feel . . . before all, to make you see."

Well, *The Cruise of the Jest* is one version of that world cruise. *The Cruise of the Fairweather* is another version, a nonfiction version, a version that is so stripped of adventure and romance that it makes truth look mundane. For the crew, life aboard *Fairweather* was, in fact, an everyday experience: they were concerned mainly with their food, the weather, cocktail hour, and fresh water showers. Their lives were structured by the recurring alternation of port and sea, of arrival and departure, and the schooner was the world they knew. And it is this world that Suttie's journal describes.

Jon Adams
Puerto Vallarta, 2013

Sausalito Boat Yard

Fairweather *was built in Georgetown, Grand Cayman in 1949. She was a traditional gaff-rigged schooner with an iron keel, a wooden hull with iron fastening, and solid wooden spars. Her length was fifty-nine feet on deck, her beam was fifteen feet, and her draft was eight feet. She had a three-cylinder GM diesel for auxiliary power. She had a 32 volt electrical system, which was used for starting the engine, and for running the navigation lights and anchor wench. She had no refrigeration, no heating, and no fresh water shower. She was built in and for the tropics.*

Introduction

Bill and Suttie Adams bought the schooner *Fairweather* in the summer of 1959. They had received a description and photos of *Fairweather* from a yacht broker, and after some hesitation, they decided to drive from San Francisco to Fort Lauderdale, Florida, to look at her. They liked the schooner, her roominess and solid structure—even her name was fitting—so they bought her on the spot and negotiated with the boat yard in For Lauderdale to have her ready for sea as soon as possible.

In December of 1959, Bill and Suttie returned to Fort Lauderdale, with their two oldest sons, Rick and Jon, and some friends, to sail *Fairweather* back to San Francisco. No one on board had any significant sailing experience, but this didn't seem to be a problem in anyone's mind. They set the sails for the first time while approaching Cuba. Then, sailing in sight of land and making jokes about Castro, Suttie, sitting aft on the taffrail, looked over the side and saw, through the clear topical water, coral heads looming up from the bottom of the sea. What followed was the first of many scenes of confusion and frantic activity that tend to plague the inexperienced or *lubber*, a word no one on board used because they were all lubbers.

Fairweather

A few days later they sailed into Port Royal, Jamaica; in fact, they had to sail into Port Royal because they had managed to use up all of their fuel. They dropped anchor off a resort owned by Anthony Jenkins, who, as it turned out, was the original owner of *Fairweather*. He had her built in Georgetown, Grand Cayman in 1949, with most of the finishing work done later in Port Royal. Anthony Jenkins' hospitality, the tropical weather (in winter), the thatched-roof bar on the edge of the bay, was all—especially after a few days sailing from Florida—an influential experience. It was what Suttie assumed cruising on a yacht was all about.

With the fuel tanks full, they left Port Royal for Panama. The course was down wind, with a heavy following sea. This sea and point of sail put *Fairweather*, with her inexperienced crew, in danger of broaching, a danger that only became fully apparent when Bill decided to set the mainsail and foresail on opposite sides of the boat, or wing-on-wing. Soon after, *Fairweather* broached to port, jibbing the foresail, which slammed across the deck, splitting the sail from leech to luff. Bill, being a quick study of his own mistakes, never sailed wing-on-wing again.

In Panama they had to buy four one-hundred foot, three inch manila lines to transit the canal. These lines were used to keep *Fairweather* in the center of the canal locks as the water was let in, and on the Pacific side, as it was let out. The pilot, who spent the day on *Fairweather* bringing her through the canal, wished them luck getting back to San Francisco. But he just shook his head in amused disbelief about the idea of sailing around the world.

The winds along the west coast of Central America and Mexico are unpredictable, but if there is any wind at all,

INTRODUCTION

it is often from the northwest. They had a vague idea of the wind conditions, and they were learning to be ready. So having run out of fuel once before, they bought four fifty-five gallon fuel drums and lashed them on deck, two to port and two to starboard at the main shrouds. In the end, they powered most of the way up the coast, pulling into ports from Costa Rica to Mexico, to take on more fuel and then to hurry on. It wasn't particularly unpleasant, but powering so much, often into a head wind, wasn't anyone's idea of cruising.

They reached San Francisco at the end of February and in the course of the next year, *Fairweather* was overhauled: rotten planks in the stern were replaced, new fuel and water tanks were added, along with a ton of lead ballast in the bilge. In the engine room, a new generator, new batteries, and a new drive shaft were added. On deck new chain plates, a new top mast, and four new working sails were added. All the paint work was stripped and repainted.

With all the work they had to do on the boat, there wasn't much time to practice their seamanship. But they did manage to spend a few hours now and then sailing on San Francisco Bay. They learned the names for all the lines, from staysail sheet to main peak-halyard, and just as important, they learned what all these lines did. Eventually they learned to set the light weather sails: the main topsail and the flying fisherman. The topsail turned out to be more work than it was worth, but the fisherman was set whenever possible: the fisherman was the last sail raised and the first one lowered. However, the confidence that this practice imparted didn't extend to the waters beyond the Golden Gate.

The Sails

Fairweather *was a gaff-rigged schooner: the mainmast was stepped aft of the foremast, and the gaff was the spar that held the upper edge of the four-sided main and foresail. Starting from the bow, the four lower or working sails were jib, staysail, foresail, and mainsail. The two upper sails were light weather sails: the topsail on the topmast and the flying fisherman between the masts. The fisherman was called "flying" because its luff was not attached to a spar or stay.* Fairweather *also carried a genoa, or large jib, which was troublesome to handle in a heavy sea, especially at the end of the bowsprit. And she carried a storm trysail, a heavy triangular sail set on the mainmast and used mainly to hove-to in a storm.*

INTRODUCTION

Although there was a lot to be done to prepare for the cruise, all the decisions and planning originated with Bill. He probably didn't have any sense of adventure, at least not of the type we associate with someone like Jack London. What he had instead was a sense of personal competitiveness that was so basic that for him it was like eating and sleeping. His approach to life was simple, even primitive: it was a question of sink-or-swim. And Bill was a swimmer. Sailing around the world was something he knew he could do because someone had already done it, and since sailing around the world was exotic—perhaps even dangerous—he wanted to do it. He wanted to show that he could do it.

Bill's attitude made the cruise possible, but it also made life on *Fairweather* often unpleasant for everyone else. At one point in her journal, Suttie associates Bill with William Bligh, but he wasn't necessarily a disciplinarian. He was more like a scientist with a lot of ideas and *Fairweather* was his laboratory and the crew his mice. In spite of this, the crew held together. Suttie's attitude, more than anything else, tempered Bill's and made life on board tolerable during the first year of the cruise. No one willing left *Fairweather* until Auckland, New Zealand, when Bill left and Suttie became the skipper.

The (initial) crew	age
Bill Adams	38
Suttie Adams	36
Rick Adams	19
Jon Adams	16
Sue Adams	12
Pat Adams	8
Verne Hansen	30
Lisa Bacelis	17

West Coast

March 4, 1961—The weather was perfect for getting underway, the sky was blue and the wind moderate. As we slipped our lines at 13:40 and powered out of the Sausalito Yacht Harbor, many of the boats in the marine gave us a sendoff with flags and horns. *Pursuit, Amarel, Hurricane, Wally & Tink,* and many other yachts escorted us out the Golden Gate. A few hours later, we were all on deck taking a last, silent look back at the San Francisco sky line—it will have to last a long time. Still, we were excited about what lay ahead, beyond the horizon.

Many have asked me why I am doing this, giving up my house and all its comforts for a life at sea. But trying to explain why I am setting out on a world cruise and heading into the unknown makes me sound a bit too idealistic. Simply put, I want to see more of the world and how other people live. I can always get another house but time creeps up on us all and a dream like this cannot be put off—or it will never be fulfilled. I like to believe that you can take away material possessions but you can't take away experiences and memories. And, of course, what an education the kids will have—at least I hope so. I think the sea will give them discipline for the future, and foreign countries will give them understanding of other people. Let's see what the next few years bring and then perhaps I'll be able to give a more definite answer.

Watches are set for two hours, with one man on watch. I drew the best watch, the six-to-eight, mornings from 06:00 to 08:00, when the sun comes up, and evenings from 18:00 to 20:00, when it goes down again. Lisa follows me with the eight-to-ten, Jon with the ten-to-twelve, Bill with the twelve-to-two, Verne with the two-to-four, and Rick with the four-to-six. Lisa was spending her weekends working on *Fairweather*, and then two weeks before our sailing date she asked if she could join us. I didn't want the responsibility of a teenage girl, but after discussing it with Bill, I decided to give her a try. She can help out below deck, and if she doesn't work out we can send her home from Mexico.

March 5—Lisa and I were the only ones who were seasick. We had steak for dinner. There won't be many of those after this. Galley duty is shared, with everyone taking a day cooking. Sue and Pat have their studies and general cleanup, but I think I'll put them on dish-washing duty when we fall into a regular routine. During the night it started to rain, and then the wind came up strong from the northwest. We averaged nine knots all night, which is just under *Fairweather's* hull speed of nine and three-quarters knots. In the morning, on my watch, I could just make out the California coast. Our first port of call is Los Angeles. Originally we had planned to make Hawaii our first port, but then we thought it wiser to take a shakedown cruise down the Mexican coast to get all the snags and wrinkles out of the boat and crew, and more important, to practice our celestial navigation.

West Coast

March 6—It was Lisa's day in the galley and she was still seasick. She would much rather make up rope, stand watch, or climb the rigging. I don't think she has slept two hours since we left. And Sue! What a worker she has turned out to be. She has been wonderful. As we came into the Santa Barbara Channel in the night, the wind was blowing strong. Jon went on watch at 22:00 and Bill told him to keep an eye out for the Anacapa Light, and also for ships, since our top-mast light wasn't working. Ten minutes later he yells down, "There's a huge light bearing down on us!" The whole crew ran up on deck expecting to see a freighter practically on top of us. But the huge light turned out to be just the moon rising in the east. Our excitement for the night wasn't over though. The wind began blowing harder and we had to lower the mainsail. This is where our inexperience shows, for we haven't mastered the art of lowering the mainsail in a strong wind without using the engine. With all the excitement, the log line was forgotten. It got caught in the propeller, so scratch one log spinner. Once we got the mainsail down, we hove-to for the night under foresail.

March 7—In the morning the wind dropped and we raised the mainsail again, but by noon there was no wind at all, and the sails began flopping as *Fairweather* rolled from side to side. It was warm. Verne took off his shoes. Lisa and I put on shorts. We waited for the wind to return, but in vain. At 13:00 we turned on the engine and powered into Los Angeles and dropped the anchor at 21:00. The ship's log read 391 miles. It was the first port on our world cruise and we needed to celebrate, especially Lisa, who just turned eighteen, so out came the gin and orange juice. Everyone felt good and content with our first passage, and now that we were in port, our mistakes at sea were forgotten. During the celebration, one of the boys would excuse himself every so often, saying he was going on deck to check the anchor. Finally curiosity got the better of Lisa and she followed Verne on deck to see what was wrong with the anchor. She returned with a red and speechless face.

March 8—In the morning we made arrangements to move over to Henry's Yacht Anchorage. It's a very nice place. It has a swimming pool, and more important, hot showers. Sue and Pat love the pool and they became whiter and whiter after each swim, as their accumulated grime washed off. Last year we met Ben and Marge Davis when they were on the *Argonaut*, and when we heard they were now in L.A., we got in touch with them. They told us the story of why they left the *Argonaut* and returned home. They just couldn't get along with the other couple in the boat's confined space, a problem that plagues many cruising boats. The day before we left, Lisa and I went shopping for fresh food. We took a sea bag, hiked a mile to the bus stop, and then rode into downtown Long Beach. We filled the sea bag with groceries, slung it over our shoulders and walked back to the bus stop along the main street. We must have been a sight. The engine was giving us some trouble, so we had some work done—replaced the injectors. It has been a pleasant week, but it's time to get moving, even if it's just to Ensenada.

March 18—We powered out of Long Beach at 08:00. As soon as we were clear of the harbor, we raised the British flag. From reports we have heard, people around the world have the idea that all Americans are rich, so instead of trying to convince them otherwise, we'll try to make them think we are British. Actually, *Fairweather* is British; she is registered in Georgetown, Grand Cayman, so the British flag is the one we should be flying. There was no wind, so we powered all the way to Ensenada and dropped the anchor at noon the next day. The log read 134 miles. Bill went to the Port Captain and got us cleared for all of Mexico—cost sixteen dollars. Verne, Lisa, and Rick went out to sample the tequila. They're still wondering how they made it back from the cantina. Rick came back first, and I sent him back for Lisa. Verne made it back just before eight in the next morning. That's the rule: everyone has to be on board by 08:00 during the week. In port the crew works on the boat until noon. They have the weekends off. The next day, in the afternoon, three Americans from a ketch in the harbor came aboard with two bottles of tequila. One of them mixed it in a big bucket with water and limes. Toward evening, as we got down toward the bottom of the bucket, we found a few matches and a cigarette lighter, but by then we didn't care much. Later, we wanted our visitors to shove off for their own boat: they were getting a little too familiar with Lisa, who seemed to enjoy the attention. Finally, Bill got out the charts and ordered the anchor raised. Our visitors took the hint. We went to bed.

March 22—We left Ensenada for Turtle Bay the next morning at 10:00. The compass heading was 160°, with the wind dead astern. On this point of sail, *Fairweather* rolls from rail-to-rail, (which made that tequila slosh around in everyone's bilge). We averaged eight to nine knots through the night, but it was impossible to sleep. My bunk is athwart ships and on the roll to starboard my head hits the aft companionway, and on the roll to port my whole body slides down to the bottom of the bunk. There is no way I can brace myself. A bunk built athwart ships sounded like a good idea when we had it put in, but now I wish I had a normal fore-and-aft bunk.

March 23—It was Verne's day in the galley. For breakfast we had pancakes with raisins, cinnamon, and hot syrup. For dinner we had some beefsteak that we bought in Ensenada—tough but tasty. Bill plotted a course that put the wind on the starboard quarter, which eased the rolling of the boat. It also took us out to sea, and at 19:00, when the log read 795 miles, we tacked back to the coast, hoping that Turtle Bay would be there in the morning. The wind was blowing strong, much stronger than it seemed because we were going with it. It took us over an hour to come about on the other tack. In the process the starboard topping-lift broke, so we lowered the mainsail. By then the wind had reached gale force strength, so we lowered the genoa and staysail and continued through the night under foresail, making five knots. I wondered if all boats have the problems we have, or if we are still just clumsy lubbers. It's a good thing we took this shakedown before attempting to cross the Pacific.

March 24—The next morning, we sighted the entrance of Turtle Bay right where it was supposed to be. We dropped the anchor at noon in the small circular bay and finally got a chance to relax. The log read 343 miles. The Port Captain came right out. He didn't want any money—just canned meat, .22 shells, and whiskey. We didn't have much experience with Mexican Port Captains, so we helped him out.

Verne was still sick—Bill too. It must have been Tequila poisoning. Everyone was in bed by 19:00. The next morning Verne was too sick to leave his bunk and Bill was feeling terrible. Later Bill got out the *Physician's Handbook* and read up on abominable pains. After studying the book and Verne's symptoms, he decided that Verne had appendicitis and that he would have to get a doctor if Verne wasn't better by noon. Verne felt much better by noon, so did Bill. I went ashore with Sue and Pat. When we looked inland, all we could see was sand, rock, and barren hills. There was not a tree, a flower, or a blade of grass anywhere. There isn't even any fresh water. The town has a salt water distillery, and each morning the people come with five gallon cans for their daily ration of water. Rick went skin diving in the kelp beds and brought back abalone for dinner.

March 26—It was Jon's day in the galley. He was still doing rice for breakfast. It's a good thing he has to do his own cleaning up. Rick baked some biscuits that made up for the rice. The wind was blowing so hard that no one went ashore. It was a peaceful day, lying around reading. For lunch we had the rest of the abalone. Sue baked a pineapple up-side-down cake. It was good.

March 27—I learned that fresh meat was available in town on Mondays, so Lisa and I went to the butcher shop, which was just a shack on the beach. Once a month a freighter drops off four cows, and each Monday one of the cows is butchered. After watching the cow being killed and chopped up with an ax, we decided we didn't need any fresh meat. The next morning we noticed that a small yacht had come into the bay. Rick and Verne rowed over and invited them for lunch. It was Herb and Joan Happoldt on the *Driftwood*. Herb told us that he built the *Driftwood* in ten months, with a hammer, a screwdriver, and saw. The boat was twenty-seven feet overall, made of plywood with oak frames (Herb said he made the frames from the packing cases that washing machines came in). The *Driftwood* has no portholes, no engine, and no head. Joan made the sails. They're on their way around the world. Good luck.

March 28—We left Turtle Bay for Cabo San Lucas at 10:00. The weather has been getting better as we sail south, and we had a fair wind. Plus, it's getting warmer, a sign of what is to come and what I picture cruising to be. Bill and Verne practiced taking sun sights with the sextant.

April 1—So far our dead reckoning has been accurate. We rounded El Arco on the west end of Cabo San Lucas, and since the bottom of the bay drops off abruptly from the beach, we dropped both anchors close-in to the beach at 10:00. The log read 420 miles. We didn't break or lose anything on our last passage, which made me think we were beginning to look more like sailors and less like lubbers. Pat and I had galley duty, and while we were clearing away the dishes, everyone else took off for shore in the dinghy. I'm not a very good swimmer, which is an exaggeration—I can't swim at all without fins. I really had to think about the situation: either I had to stay confined to the boat, or I had to get in the water and swim ashore. The water in Cabo is astonishingly clear, but Barbara on the *Escaped* told us that there were sharks in the bay. I decided to try to swim ashore anyway. Pat and I jumped in the water and Pat took off in a hurry—so that a shark couldn't get him. He reached the beach in record time, then being a nice guy, he came back to help me as I huffed and puffed through the water.

Afterwards it was a good feeling, knowing I could do it. And then the first thing I noticed on the beach was shark vertebra scattered everywhere. Bill was certainly surprised to see us ashore. The next day was Easter and there were no eggs to be had in the village. Barbara said we could try to get some from the *Goodwill,* a hundred-and-fifty foot schooner, so we rowed over to ask Mr. Laraby if he had any eggs. He met us with a big smile and a double scotch—one for each of us. After the tour of the boat and the scotch, it became difficult to remember what we were there for, but we must have mentioned eggs at some point because I had a whole crate of them when I got back to *Fairweather.* For the next week we had a lot of huevos fritos, huevos mexicanos, and huevos rancheros.

April 6—Around midnight Bill went on deck to check the anchor—both of them—before turning in. So by chance he saw that the *Vallerie Queen* with Don Stewart and his crew had just anchored in the bay. They were planning to sneak over, board us, and throw us all in the water (so they told us later). But we saw them first. Grabbing some gin, we rowed over to them while they were trying to get their long boat in the water. At the height of the merrymaking, they challenged us to a race to Mazatlán, with the losing captain having to put in ten hours work on the winning boat. Then Don swept his arm across the cabin table, wiping it clean of bottles and glasses—that's why we were on his boat—and challenged Rick to an arm-wrestling match. Rick won. While Bill was on deck, someone pushed him overboard, which started a melee. It's a wonder someone didn't drown. I think we won because they never got Rick over the side. He climbed up the main mast to the cross-

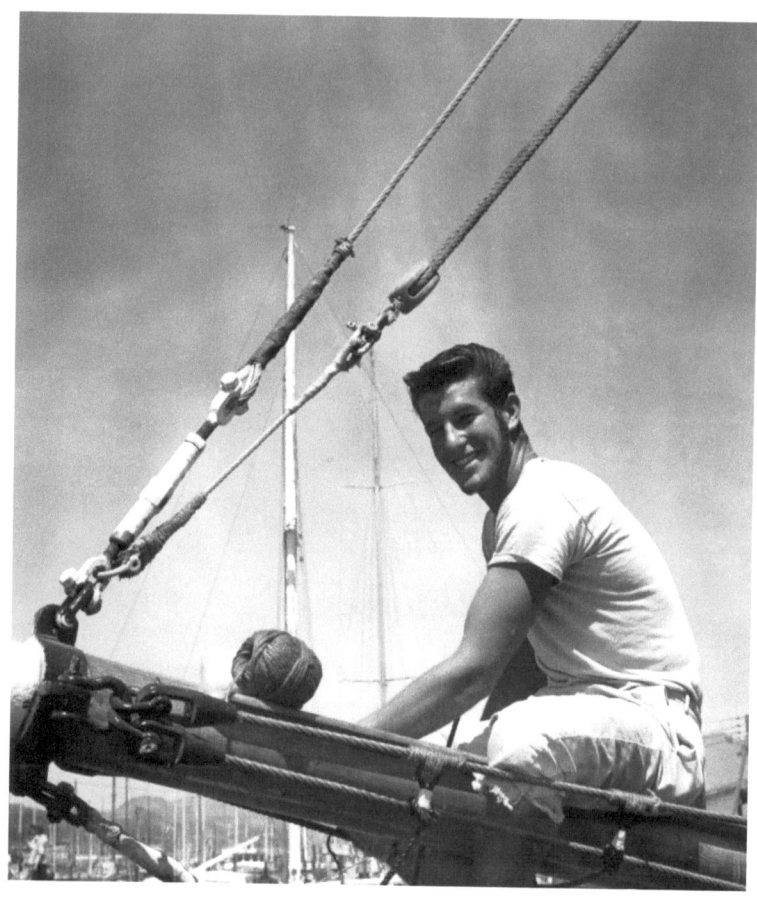

Rick

While getting Fairweather *ready for her world cruise, Rick did most of the rigging work, from stepping a new topmast to splicing new shrouds. Here he is finishing the netting under the bowsprit by serving the jack stays.*

trees where no one could reach him. At 04:30 we decided it was time to leave. It was then that we noticed someone must have landed in our dinghy because it was floating upside down.

April 7—With some of the other yachts in the bay, including *Karana* with Fred and Pearl Wittle, and *Watoridori* with George and Sonya Holland, we bought a pig and roasted it on the beach. Fred got the pig for sixteen dollars and did the roasting. Fred is a retired Navy chief and loves the sea. Pearl loves Fred. Don Stewart arrived with his arm in a sling and tape across his nose. His crew had some cuts and bruises showing here and there. In the evening we ate the pig with chili beans, baked potatoes, tossed salad, tortillas, and lots of Carta Blanc to wash it all down. George and Sonja missed out. There was a heavy surge in the bay and the *Watoridori* kept dragging her anchor. It must have been embarrassing for George, with everyone on the beach watching him drag his 35 pound kedge all over the place. We had out both our 250 pound fisherman and our 65 pound kedge, and they were holding fast.

April 8—*Driftwood* sailed into the bay and said that there had been a storm out at sea, which was the cause of the heavy surge. By now Cabo San Lucas was beginning to look like a yacht club for cruising boats: *Watoridori, Karana, Vallerie Queen, Driftwood,* and *Fairweather.* There was even a welcoming committee: Mario. Every time we landed on the beach with our dinghy, Mario, who was about eight years old, would run down and help pull it out of the surf. He would clean it out and then sit in it and guard it. He lived in a shack on a sand dune above the beach, so he always knew when we were coming ashore. I had some new orange nylon rugs for the stern and main cabins made before we left San Francisco, but they turned out to be impractical on the boat—hard to clean and usually wet. So one morning I brought the rugs ashore and gave them to Mario.

April 10—This was the morning of the big race to Mazatlán. We raised anchor at 08:00 and left Cabo half-an-hour before the *Vallerie Queen* and half-an-hour after *Karana*, who had also entered the race. Just beyond the bay, a large patch of water was broken and confused by some commotion below the surface. As we sailed through the patch, we saw that it was a feeding frenzy: thousands of small fish were being eaten by tuna, and in turn, the tuna were being eaten by sharks. Blood was everywhere. We thought that this was a good opportunity to catch a tuna, so Rick threw over the fish-line. We sailed right through the middle of the frenzy but didn't catch a thing. Later, as we passed *Karana*, Fred held up a tuna that must have been thirty to forty pounds. The *Vallerie Queen* was about a mile astern all day. We were worried that the *Queen* would out sail us. She is a Herreschoff design, and although like *Fairweather*, she's a gaff-rigged schooner, at 68 feet she's ten feet longer, with a narrower beam and a deeper draft. This adds up to a faster boat. A few months ago, coming through the Golden Gate, we beat her in, but that was because there was a strong wind and our sails were new—Don was afraid of blowing out his old sails. So for the race to Mazatlán, we wanted a strong wind because we could carry more canvass for much longer. But what we got was a light wind that moved us along at three to four knots. We had everything up, our four working sails, plus our two light-weather sails:

the topsail and the flying fisherman. Through our binoculars we watched with envy as the *Queen* set one light-weather sail after another, some of which we had never seen before: a big drifter and even a gollywobbler. The best we could do was rig our storm trysail under the main boom as a kind of stud sail—Verne called it our water sail. But at dusk the *Queen* was still a mile astern. We doused our running lights, just in case the *Queen* was depending on our navigation. During the night the wind dropped, so that by morning we were making just two knots. At first light we looked for the *Queen,* and there she was on the horizon, still astern. As we drifted along, a thirty-foot whale shark came up under our stern. We were surprised to see this shy, plankton-eating monster. It had a blue shark acting as a pilot fish. Later we spotted what looked like rocks floating in the water, and then we realized that they were sea turtles. Rick caught one, and we had turtle steaks for lunch and Chili con Tortuga for dinner.

April 12—We passed the lighthouse at the entrance to Mazatlán after midnight, and anchored in the marina with the sport-fishing fleet at 01:00. The log read 183 miles. We were so sure the *Queen* was right behind us that we stayed up for two hours waiting for her. She didn't show up, so Verne and Lisa slept on deck to keep her crew from sneaking aboard. The *Karana* came in at 09:00 that morning, and then the *Queen* came in at noon. Captain Stewart came aboard and gave us five minutes to gloat, so Bill took his five minutes in two-second intervals. We wrapped up a bottle of Tequila, and Verne printed up a certificate that read: "Presented to the Second best Schooner in the Three-Boat Yacht Race from Cabo San Lucas to Mazatlán,

1961." The presentation ceremony was interrupted with the sporadic gloating of the winning captain.

April 14—When we arrived in Mazatlán, the 30-foot cutter *Herta* was anchored in the harbor. Heinz and Herta came on deck at 06:00 that morning, preparing to sail back to San Diego, mainly because they were bored with Mazatlán—there were no other yachts to visit and swap stories with. But when they saw the *Fairweather,* they decided to stay at least another day. Then the *Karana* came in. Fred and Pearl on the *Karana* were also from San Diego and good friends of Heinz and Herta. So the *Herta* didn't leave.

April 16—Sunday was a lovely, sunny, lazy day, which meant it was a good day to have friends aboard. So we called out to the *Herta* and *Karana* that cocktails were being served in ten minutes. Before the day was over, there was a real swinging party on board. Whenever there is a party on board a yacht, it's like open house, in which people get a chance to meet and talk. Around midnight we all ended up at the Hotel Belmar on Playa Olas Altas, where we had dinner. The streak was terrific and the prices were better—23 pesos. Speaking of food prices, I went into town to the Mercado to do some grocery shopping and had a comida corrida that included sopa, birria (stew), arroz, frijoles, pan y mantequilla, and melón, all for four pesos. We found showers right on the beach. In every port showers are important because there is no shower on the *Fairweather*—can't have everything on a boat. The showers on the beach are two pesos, which includes a rub down. Lisa and I went over and we thought the guy who was running the showers was ok, until Lisa caught him looking at her with some fixed mirrors. Lisa told him that looking was

West Coast

going to cost him some money—and collected 40 pesos from him. The *Vallerie Queen* left today, and we cheered her as she got underway. Everyone on the *Queen* seemed to be having a great time. But unfortunately, no work was getting done on the boat. Since the crew members are paying their way, Don can't order them about to do the sanding and painting that the *Queen* sadly needs.

April 18—The *Watoridori* came in yesterday and was dragging her anchor within two hours. Rick and I went over to help her, and then I fell overboard from the dinghy—disgusting. Her two crew members jumped ship, so George and Sonya will be sailing by themselves. George never uses his sails anyway, he just powers everywhere. I guess they won't have any problems. Sue and Pat insisted that *Fairweather* needed a parrot, so we bought one at the Mercado for six pesos, including the bamboo cage it was in. We named the parrot Mario, after the boy on the beach in Cabo.

April 21—We picked up fresh bread, fruit, and vegetables and set sail for Isla María Madre at 10:00. The compass course was 173° and following us was our small flotilla: *Karana*, *Herta*, and *Driftwood*. We reached María Madre at noon the next day. The log read 95 miles. María Madre is a prison colony for federal convicts. Visitors are not allowed on the island without a guide, and they must be off the island by 18:00. Dinghies can be landed only at the pier—not on the beach. When we went ashore we were met by a guide, who told us within the first 15 minutes why he was sent to the island. He had killed a priest—forty years ago. He explained how the prison worked. There are about 300 prisoners. They have the freedom of the town but they must be in their cells or huts by 18:00. Those prisoners who can afford it can buy a plot of land, build a house—really just a hut—and bring their families over from the mainland. They must work at least two hours a day for the prison. The fortunate ones have jobs in the rope factory or the tortilla factory and earn one peso a day. There is a movie once a week. The General in command of the colony is both respected and liked. He has built a hospital and a pier, planted fruit trees, and made the living conditions as pleasant as possible. Our guide was very proud of the hospital and insisted on showing it to us. He introduced us to one of the patients, whose hand had been cut off. He said there was a mad killer who had terrorized the prison for seven years and who had killed ten prisoners during that time. Five men decided to put a stop to him, and so they attacked him with machetes. They chopped off his head, but in the fight the mad killer managed to kill one of them and cut the hand off of another, the one who was telling us the story.

April 22—The next morning our dinghy was gone. We didn't know if it had broken loose or if a prisoner had stolen it, in an attempt to escape to the mainland. We assumed that it had probably just broken loose, so Bill worked out the direction the drift and wind would carry it and we raised the anchor and set sail to look for it. Verne was up on the crosstrees and four hours later he spotted it. Coming up on the dinghy, we were prepared to find it occupied, but it was, much to our relief, empty. When we returned to María Madre, we anchored next to the *Karana*. The swimming is terrific, the water is warm and clear. We were told in the town that it was dangerous to swim because of the sharks, but we assumed that was just to frighten the prisoners. Later we went over to the *Karana* for rum and lime. Heinz and Joan were in a heated argument about Mexicans. Heinz claimed that the Mexicans were a lazy race. Joan lived in Mexico for five years and she had a great respect and admiration for the Mexicans. I think Heinz's German background was showing through in his argument. Anyway, he was getting so excited that his accent got thicker and thicker until no one could understand what he was saying.

April 24—Our small flotilla of yachts decided to leave this morning for María Cleofas, the southernmost island of the Tres Marías—a distance of 28 miles. We sailed off the anchor at 10:00, and while passing María Magdalena in the middle of the island chain, somehow the chart got turned upside down. The chart showed a reef that we had to watch out for, but as we followed the coast of María Cleofas, looking for the anchorage, we couldn't see either the reef or the anchorage. Then, coming about, we suddenly saw the reef—we had sailed right over it. Finally we spotted the *Karana* and *Herta* at anchor and sailed in to join them. Fred and Heinz both said that they thought we were goners when they saw us heading toward the reef. It seems we were lucky that time. I went below to make some coffee but the pump was dry. There was no water. We turned on the other water tank, but it was empty too. A copper water-pipe had come lose and all our fresh water had drained into the bilge. We had to use the thirty gallons of emergency water that we carried in a barrel on deck. The Sailing Directions say that there is a fresh water spring on the island, so we'll investigate in the morning. Since we

Puerto Vallarta

A view of Puerto Vallarta from the Rio Cuale, where Suttie washed the her laundry. A woman in the distance is carrying her laundry on her head. The tower of the church, La Iglesia de Nuestra Señora de Guadalupe, can be seen in the background. The church didn't receive its famous crown until 1963, two years after Fairweather *visited Banderas Bay.*

lost sight of the *Driftwood* during the day, we left our topmast light on to direct them in. Then we all took a swim before turning in.

April 25—In the morning we went ashore and found the island deserted, except for very friendly birds and iguanas. I was walking along the beach with Sue and Pat when a duckish looking bird waddled up to us. We thought we had inadvertently captured a unique bird, and since we didn't want it to get away as we continued exploring, we tied it to a rock with one of Pat's shoe-strings. Soon afterwards we felt rather silly when we discovered that all the birds would walk right up to us. I quickly sent Pat back to release our poor shoe-string-bound friend. Moving from the open beach into the tree-covered jungle felt strange. It was near the end of the dry season, so there wasn't much undergrowth, and the leaves rustled under our feet. The sunlight through the trees, together with the silence, once away from the sound of the surf, was uncanny. And then a large iguana dropped from a tree and landed just in front of us. It was more than four feet long and after giving us a look of disdain, it moved off into the trees. Like the bird that first walked up to us, an iguana dropping from a tree was not a singular event. Later, Fred caught a few iguanas. He said the tails were good to eat. He skinned the tails and cut them into bite size pieces, and then he marinated the pieces with lime and onions. In the evening he barbecued them on skewers. Not everyone tried them. Since it was the end of the dry season, the fresh water spring described in the Sailing Directions was completely dried up. So we are leaving in the morning for Banderas Bay and Puerto Vallarta. Still haven't seen the *Driftwood*.

Yalapa Anchorage

The "small flotilla" anchored at Yalapa. The yachts from left to right are Herta, Karana, Driftwood, *and* Fairweather. *Although the bay at Yalapa was well protected, it was a difficult anchorage because the bottom of the bay was steep and dropped off rapidly from the shore.*

West Coast

April 25—We sailed off the anchor and headed for Puerto Vallarta at 14:00. While sailing into Banderas Bay, we saw giant manta rays leaping into the air. Later we learned that April was their mating season. Ever since Turtle Bay the weather and winds have been perfect for sailing. We've had the engine on only twice and that was entering and leaving Mazatlán. I like to think that we are becoming better sailors, but I think it's mainly the good sailing weather that has made everything seem like weekend cruising. We sailed into Puerto Vallarta the next day and anchored off the beach at 11:00. The log read 68 miles. There is no harbor here and the boats are at the mercy of the swell. *Fairweather* rolls from port to starboard, sometimes from rail-to-rail. *Karana* and *Herta* spent a night in a small protected harbor on the south side of the bay, and after seeing the anchorage at Puerto Vallarta, they wished they had stayed there—*Driftwood* was here. Going ashore in the dinghy is either exhilarating or disastrous, depending on our skill and luck. Either we catch a wave just right and ride it into the beach, or the wave catches us and flips the dinghy over. Once the dinghy flipped over and caught Jon underneath. He couldn't get out from under it until I ran down the beach and lifted it off of him. Bill wanted him to try and get it off by himself, but there are times when I just don't listen to him.

I noticed that all the local women did their laundry in the Río Cuale, so I took mine there. Each woman has her own private place, with a rock and a palm-leaf roof for shade. I found an unoccupied place and started at it. I was doing fine until I saw a pile of shit floating toward me. Glancing up I saw that I was just downstream from where the bur-

Yalapa Waterfall

Suttie bathing in Yalapa. In time, the crew became used to bathing at sea in salt water, but even so, a fresh water shower, even under the cold spring water of a waterfall, was a luxury that was never passed up.

ros crossed the river. Every time they step in the water they stop to piss and shit. So I had to move upstream. Then all I had to deal with was an occasional dead rat or dog. After hours of scrubbing and rinsing in fresh water, my wash day wasn't over—I had to get the clean laundry back to the *Fairweather*, which meant negotiating the surf. Jon, who was getting better at judging the waves, missed this one and flipped the dinghy again, and as a result the laundry got soaked with salt water. I just hung it up that way.

April 29—We sailed off the anchor at 11:00 and headed for Yelapa on the southern rim of Banderas Bay. It was only fifteen miles as the dolphin swims, but it was seven hours of tacking back and forth before we could drop anchor at Yelapa. The anchorage is small and deep, with the bottom dropping off sharply from the beach. The *Herta* and *Karana* were already here, and we had to put out a stern anchor to keep from swinging into them. The view here is tropical: it's a different Mexico from the north, especially Baja with its dry and somewhat bleak desert scenery. Yelapa is how I imagine the islands in the South Sea will look, with houses made of palm leaves and dense green trees and vines coming right down to the shore. When I get to the South Seas I must remember to make a comparison.

Each morning a fisherman stops by and sells us a large red snapper for five pesos. Forty pounds of bananas cost ten pesos. With the crew each taking a day in the galley, we are having a variety of meals. Verne is an excellent cook: it isn't so much what he cooks but the little things he adds to it. Rick is good, Lisa does alright, and Jon is improving. Bill has his own ideas on what a meal should consist of and all his meals taste the same. Sue and Pat do the evening dishes, so galley duty really isn't too much of a chore.

There are some Americans living in the hills around here. They seem to spend most of their time drinking riceca—made from cactus—and smoking pot. Their nominal leader is Golden Boy, a guy with golden hair, golden beard, and a gold earring. A new bar-restaurant-nightclub-dance-hall just opened—the only one in the village—so we all went to the opening night. The food was a disappointment—bistec that was greasy and tough. Then when the dancing started, we found that we had to pay to dance. It didn't matter who the man danced with, during the dance a guy came around on the dance floor and collected two pesos. Verne wanted to stay longer, so we left the dinghy on the beach for him and rowed out with Fred and Pearl. This morning Verne was on the beach calling for the dinghy—he hadn't noticed that he had slept next to it all night. As I said, the food last night was a disappointment—that was an understatement. We all—Bill, Jon, Lisa, and me—have a case of Montezuma's Revenge. The best place to take a fresh water bath is to follow the stream up to a small pool with a waterfall. It's cold but refreshing. *Driftwood* arrived. It took them three days to make fifteen miles against the wind.

May 5—We powered out of Yelapa for Manzanillo at 11:00. *Herta* left earlier, heading back to San Diego. Once out of Yelapa, we raised the sails, and picking up speed, we passed *Karana* before clearing Cabo Corrientes, the south cape of Banderas Bay. Just before midnight, Jon jibed the main in light airs, and in the confusion that followed, he then jibed it back again. With the second jibe the boom-bail broke and the heavy main-sheet block crashed through the skylight over the aft-cabin, just missing Pat. Verne cut his feet running through the broken glass on the cabin floor. And as Rick ran forward on deck, he got knocked down by the fore-boom. We took down all the sails—the wind had died all together—and with huge swells from the west rolling us from rail-to-rail—we powered through the night. The next morning we were getting low on fuel, so the crew jury-rigged the main-sheet and set sail again. We made only ten miles in the light wind. At sunset, Bill estimated we had just enough fuel to make the last ten miles into port. We anchored in Manzanillo at 21:00 with just two inches of fuel left in the tank—most of it sludge. The log read 148 miles.

It says in the logbook that we spent ten days in Manzanillo, but I can't imagine what we did during that time. Manzanillo is a major port and the harbor is filthy with oil. There is nothing touristy about town, although it has a large and fascinating Mercado and beer is only sixteen pesos per case. I've decided that if Lisa doesn't change her general attitude, I'll have to send her home from Acapulco. I haven't said anything about her because there isn't anything I can put my finger on or accuse her of—she just gets on everyone's nerves, not just mine. Other boat people have asked how she gets along on the boat because they have felt the same thing about her. Maybe she'll change.

May 16—We sailed off the anchor and headed for Zihautanejo. In the light winds we set everything, including the topsail and fisherman. We were sailing along pleasantly when the shackle broke on the topsail halyard and the block fell to the deck, just missing Rick.

May 17—The wind picked up during the day and we took down the mainsail at 15:00, a maneuver we still seem to be fumbling with. We broke another lazy-jack. With just the foresail up, we entered the bay at Zihautanejo after nightfall. There was no moon and we didn't have a harbor chart, which made piloting into the anchorage a little risky. Luckily all the navigation lights in the harbor were working. All I can say is that, if I were the skipper, we would have hove-to at the entrance of the bay and waited for daylight.

May 18—As I looked out of the aft-hatch in the morning, the land-locked bay of Zihautanejo made me think of what Acapulco must have looked like before it became a famous tourist resort. You know the clams are fresh here because when you order them at a beach-side cafe, a diver comes out of the water with a sack full and opens them in front of you. If they wiggle when you squeeze lime on them, then they are ok. We met a group of Mexicans who were down from Mexico City: Paco—the leader—Ruben, and Kiri. They were here buying property to develop into a tourist resort. They seem to mix their work and play to the point where you can't tell when they ever work. Paco invited us to sit at his table during the local fiesta in the plaza. His table ran the entire length of the square and it was loaded down with fruit and rum. Joan from the *Driftwood* surprised us. We were used to seeing her in Herb's old clothes, hair all tangled and no lipstick on, but when she arrived all made up and ready to party, she was a knock out. On the other side of the square there was another long table with another crowd from Mexico City. They began asking Lisa and me to dance frequently, and then all of a sudden Paco says "Let's go." So we went back to *Fairweather* and the party went on until five in the morning. When we all finally fell asleep, Paco and his crowd left. Later I asked why we left the fiesta in such a hurry. It seems that Paco and his crowd were getting upset because the other crowd from Mexico City was asking Lisa and me to dance. And since all the Mexicans carry pistols in their back pocket, Paco decided it was better to leave before trouble started. I wonder what kind of racket Paco and his crowd are in.

Ruben, one of Paco's men, has been making a play for Lisa. I was told he was married and had three children. I repeated this to Lisa, but I guess she didn't believe me. One afternoon she left the boat and didn't return all night. The next morning I met her on the quay. She was all smiles, saying she and Ruben were married. I said I didn't see how that could be possible, and she said that Ruben told her he wasn't married. So then I asked her who married them, and she said that Herb, as Captain of the *Driftwood*, did. She went on to say that Ruben was picking her up this afternoon and taking her to Mexico City. I was ready to believe that when I saw it happen—which I never did. I feel sorry for Lisa but she is past the age to change her ways. I know now for sure that she is going home from Acapulco.

May 24—We left Zihautanejo for Acapulco at 09:00, with fair but light winds. Kiri, one of Paco's men, wanted to sail with us to Acapulco, so we gave him a bunk and a locker for his gear. Bill told him he had to put his gun in the locker too. I asked Kiri if he had ever shot anyone and he said yes. Then I asked him if he had even been shot himself and he said yes, twice. He showed me the two scars, one on his left hand and the other on his upper arm. We have been trailing a fishing line with a yellow-feathered lure, and this morning we caught a big tuna. So for lunch we had fried tuna sandwiches and for dinner fried tuna steaks. I think I could get to like fish, if it always tastes this good.

    May 25—We sailed into Acapulco at 11:00. The log read 125 miles. It's good to be here and know that we will stay for a while. The first thing on my to-do list is to get Lisa on her way home. We took her off our papers when we went to the Port Captain. I haven't written anything about her because she has been so upsetting. In fact she has been downright disgusting. On board she thinks only of herself. In port we have to apologize for her and explain that she isn't our daughter. After her affair in Zihautanejo, we all decided that we had had enough, not only Bill and I, but the rest of the crew as well. The boys even refuse to go ashore with her anymore. It was very hard for me to tell her she was going home, but it had to be done. And I told her why. I still don't know whether she is as stupid as she seems or if it's all pretense. I won't go into what she was really like, but all around she made a very poor crew member. This has been reinforced by the fact that it is so pleasant on board now without her.

    We are anchored off the yacht club, but we still have to pay a hundred pesos a week to use the club facilities, which is well worth it. Sue and Pat like the swimming pool, and I can give them their school lessons upstairs. We met Howard Taylor and his family at the club: Myra, Tommy, Chris, Allen, and Layton. They are getting their forty-foot ketch ready to leave for the Marquesas in about a week. After some fast talking on their part, Bill and I decided to change our plans of sailing to Panama and the Galápagos, and instead to head straight for the Marquesas. But we can't leave for another month because of all the preparations we have to make. I'm still wondering how we got talked into sailing to the Marquesas, but we have to make an ocean passage sometime and now is as good a time as any.

June 1—At the yacht club, they said the rainy season starts on June first and sure enough, early in the morning of June first it started to rain and rain hard.

We decided to take a trip to Mexico City. Bill and I went into town to rent a car. All seven of us went, leaving *Fairweather* in the care of Fred and Pearl Wittle on the *Karana*. The road to Mexico City is a good one. The only problem is the cows, horses, pigs, burros, and goats also seem to think it's a good one. We nearly clipped a few of them. It was an interesting drive—all seven hours of it. We stopped at Nancy Harris' house. Nancy sailed with us from Zihautanejo to Acapulco, and she offered to put us up if we were ever in Mexico City, but she wasn't home. After some hesitation, we looked up the La Frontera, Paco's nightclub. Now I know what he does for a living. He owns a nightclub outside the city, where he runs a "house." He and his wife gave us the best apartment during our stay. And they sent one of their cousins with us to see the pyramids and tombs of Montezuma, but after four days in a big city, we were ready to return to the *Fairweather*. Paco and his wife were really wonderful—if only the brass band didn't play so loud all night.

With our first ocean passage in front of us, I had to plan carefully the ordering of our provisions. When I ordered in San Francisco, I just made out a basic menu for one month and then multiplied the amount of food we needed for one month by six. I've kept a checklist of the food we have used since leaving San Francisco, so I was able to reorder what we needed. Plus, the cruise down to Acapulco gave me a good idea of what was good and what wasn't. Even without refrigeration, the canned meat is holding up well, but there never seem to be enough sweet things, such as cookies and cake-mixes.

The table in the main cabin has proven to be very impractical. It was impossible to set up for a meal in a rough sea, so Bill had a gimbaled table made out of thick mahogany. What a difference it makes. We traded the old table to the *Dwen Wynn* for a gallon of canned mashed potatoes.

July 3—At half past four in the morning there was a knock on the aft-hatch. We were all sleeping below deck because of the rain. I stuck my head out to see who it was. It turned out to be a young women called Adel. She said in a desperate voice, "I want to come with you. Please, let me come with you!" I told her to come below and have a cup of coffee. I explained to her that we were headed for Tahiti. She didn't know or care where that was—she just wanted to get out of Acapulco. Then she said the magic words: she liked to cook. She had no place to sleep, so I said she could stay on board for a few days, and we would see how things worked out.

July 6—We took *Fairweather* over to the ways at the naval yard, had her hauled out, and her bottom covered with anti-fouling paint. We are loaded with food, water, and fuel, and now we are ready for the passage to the Marquesas. As for Adel, our early morning visitor, she is working out fine. She can cook. As a Panamanian she knows how to deal with the people at the Mercado, and so far she has saved us half of our food bill. Since she still wants to come with us, I told her we would take her as far as Tahiti.

Sailing West

From Acapulco, Fairweather *headed southwest to Nuku Hive Island in the Marquesas of French Polynesia, a distance of approximately 3,000 miles. Crossing the Pacific to the Marquesas gave the crew the sense that they were really cruising. It also gave them confidence in their seamanship and navigation.*

South Seas

July 8—16:00 and we are abeam Acapulco light, on our way to the Marquesas. This is it. Sailing down the coast from San Francisco to Acapulco gave us some experience and confidence for our first ocean passage. We have always been close to land, so that we could make for a port if something went wrong. Now we are on our own. No ports until the Marquesas. We were under full sail, then at about 21:00 we were hit by a heavy squall and had to reef down. Oh, was I seasick. I read somewhere that a squall was a good time to take a fresh water shower. It must have been an old sea story. I can't imagine going on deck in such a black and cold night, with the deck rolling and pitching so much that you have to hold on with both hands. That's a hard way to take a shower.

July 9—It's been one squall after another, but we made 132 miles in the first twenty-four hours. At sundown we were racing along at eight knots, so we decided to take in the genoa and reef the mainsail for the night. I turned into the wind, while the boys handled the sails, but when I turned back on course there was no wind. But it's a good thing we reefed down because during the night a storm blew up. No squall this time but the full gale.

July 10—It's still blowing hard and we are sailing under reefed main and foresail. What a mess below deck. Everything is wet. But just think how nice it will be when the weather clears. Adel, our new Panamanian cook, is seasick. She tried hard the first two days out of Acapulco, but today she just gave up. Tonight the storm has become worse and we are hove-to under foresail. We all went below, ate dinner and then went to bed.

July 11—There is still a heavy overcast and we are unable to take a sun sight, so we are still depending on dead reckoning to plot our position. The wind was calmer this morning, but as soon as we shook out the reefs, *bang*—another gale hit us. We double reefed the main and foresail again and continued on our way. Compass course 180°. Adel came up smiling this morning, feeling good. But by the end of the day she was ready to swim back to Acapulco. She hasn't caught the knack yet of cooking on a two-burner stove in a rolling and pitching galley. I think she rather regrets coming now. The gimbaled table works fine, even in a heavy sea.

July 12—The sky is still overcast but not quite so dark. We had breakfast at 10:00, because the cook is still fighting the galley. Rick went up on deck and came running below screaming, "The sun, the sun. I see the sun." Verne put on his dark glasses—what excitement. It didn't end there. The jib halyard parted, and Rick had to climb to the top of the foremast and set up a new halyard at the masthead, while I tried to keep the boat steady—no small feat. As soon as he got the new halyard rove, the foresail ripped at the leech. What fun.

July 13—The sun has been breaking through the overcast all morning. Astern the horizon is dark with storm clouds. We brought our bedding and clothes on deck to dry them out. Everyone is over their seasickness. What a difference a little sun makes.

July 14—We made good time last night, with *Fairweather* averaging eight and half knots. Two squalls hit us on my watch this morning. At least I got my face washed.

July 15— One week out of Acapulco and the log reads 653 miles. The first four days I'd given anything to be sitting at home (wherever that is) in an easy chair with a drink in my hand, talking about sailing. But now I am looking forward to the rest of the passage.

July 16—Our cook decided she was going to take the day off. Being as she is a good cook, though rather temperamental, we thought we had better humor her. We did ask her what would happen if everyone on board decided to take the day off, but it didn't seem to make an impression on her. What a lovely, sunny day. Adel, Sue, and I chased the men below and then we stripped down to take a salt water bath. I know we are supposed to take fresh water showers during rain squalls, but who wants to be running around in the nude trying to wash at a time like that. Today we were all supposed to get our grog, but I guess everyone was just talking about it because no one really wanted any. The ocean must be stimulating enough.

July 17—We are in the doldrums now. We have been averaging 100 miles a day, so that puts us one quarter of the way to the Marquesas.

July 18—We were hit by another storm and had to run under reefed main and foresail. Then both the main and

School at Sea

Sue and Pat continued their school work at sea. On land they attended school in such ports as Papeete, Tahiti and Rhodes, Greece. Although their schooling was at times intermittent, they had no problem in high school when they returned to San Francisco at the end of the world cruise. In the photo, Suttie watches from the helm as Jon reads to Sue and Pat.

foresail ripped. The crew spent eight hours with the needle and palm repairing them—in the rain.

July 19—There hasn't been any sun for two days, so we haven't been able to take any sun sights. Our dead reckoning puts us close to 5° north. With this weather, it doesn't seem that we were that close to the equator. Maybe this is normal weather here.

July 20—For breakfast we had Mexican scrambled eggs, fried rice, and squid. The eggs and rice were good but that squid tasted just like it looked, squiddy. Now I know what Adel was doing on deck this morning: picking up squid that had hit the sails and fallen on deck. I only hope we don't go through another school of them. Then we had squid for lunch. Everyone is still hungry, except Adel. She likes squid. They may be good but not the way she prepares them.

July 21—Today is truly the first beautiful day we've had. We are now in the southeast trades. Noon position:

Lat. 119° 30" W
Long. 1° 40" N
Log 1461 miles

This is really wonderful sailing. Everyone is on deck enjoying the sun. Verne got out his conga drum and Adel began to dance. She said she learnt to dance in a convent in Cuba, but it looks more like she learnt it in a strip show. Adel told me one evening while I was on watch that she was a high-class professional prostitute. Not having met a prostitute before—high-class or otherwise—I had to take her word for it. On the boat she behaves herself, and I like her.

July 22—We nearly ran into a whale today. It was lying on the surface, right on our course. The helmsman saw it just in time to avert a collision. Our position at noon:

Lat. 121° 21" W
Long. 0° 35" N
Log 1612 miles

This means that tonight around midnight we will cross the equator. The way we are all looking forward to it, you would think the "line" is something to see.

July 23—Today we celebrated crossing the equator. The weather was beautiful and balmy, as Big Daddy Neptune climbed up over the bow, wearing a red tam, dark glasses, a spaghetti string beard, and big, baggy pants. In one hand he was carrying an old broom with its straw tied into a trident, and in his other hand he was carrying a big bag of goodies. We each had to kneel down in front of him while he drew an anchor on our forehead with lipstick and mumbled a few "sacred" words. Then he baptized us with a bucket of sea water (which was colder than I expected), and that transformed us from Pollywogs into Shellbacks. After the baptism, we got some grog. Big Daddy Neptune got his turn because he was a Pollywog too. In fact Big Daddy Neptune celebrated his baptism so much that he ended up in his bunk and couldn't even come to dinner.

July 25—This is South Sea cruising. This is what you read about in the books. We saw mahi-mahi following the boat all day. We tried everything we could think of to catch one but we had no luck. I read in Heyerdahl's *Kon-Tiki* that they used flying fish for bait, so when the next one landed on deck, it went on the hook. That didn't work at all because we are making seven and a half knots, and in no time there was nothing left of the bait on the hook. I made four pies for dinner (It was Adel's "day off"). I thought I'd save my piece for my morning watch. I should have known better.

July 26—I baked fresh bread today in a heavy kettle on top of the stove. It was highly successful. Today we threw another empty rum bottle overboard with a note in it. How interesting it would be if someday someone turns up with one of our notes. Speaking of empty rum bottles, it seems as if they are emptying rather fast, considering none of us are big drinkers. This morning I found out where the rum was going, and also why breakfast is so late every morning. There was Adel standing in the galley, trying to cook with a cigarette in one hand and a glass of rum in the other. I thought it looked funny as hell, but the Captain didn't see it that way and a lot of unpleasant words were said. The Captain has the temperament of a William Bligh, with a little bit of his own William thrown in. Poor Adel. The rum was taken out of the galley and stowed away in the stern cabin.

July 27—We are 625 miles from Nuku Hiva. The first land we sight will be Ua Huka, an island to the east of Nuku Hiva. Our navigators predict that we will be able to see Ua Huka on the 30th. When we left Acapulco, I put two silver dollars on the bulletin board for whoever sights land first.

July 30—Noon. We sighted Ua Huka Island under a layer of thick clouds. It was dead ahead. Our navigators are very proud of themselves and they have every right to be. None of them has done any off-shore navigation before,

Bill

Bill was the Captain of Fairweather from San Francisco to Auckland, New Zealand. In the photo, Bill is tightening the main peak halyard, while getting underway in Nuku Hiva. The people of Nuku Hiva gave each crew member a lei made from the Tiare of Tahiti. The flower behind his left ear means that he is taken. But the crew learned that only later.

and they have brought *Fairweather* three thousand miles across the Pacific to a six by eight mile island. We sighted Nuku Hiva at 18:00. Naturally it was our luck to approach port at night, but this time we reduced sail and hove-to under foresail until morning. And who won the silver dollars? I think there might have been a little hanky-panky but Pat got them. It was a good passage. We find we all get along well, with everyone doing their share of the work. Of course we are all a little subdued by the overbearing personality of the Captain. Time will tell.

July 31—We sailed into Taiohae Bay in Nuka Hiva and anchored at 11:00. The log read 2,810 miles. We were 23 days at sea, averaging 122 miles a day. The Captain went ashore to clear and get visas to stay in French Polynesia. The regular procedure before coming to the Marquesas is to go to a French Consulate and get a visa to enter French Polynesia, which involves putting up a bond of $200 per person. We didn't get visas before coming because we thought it was an added expense and quite unnecessary. Verne was very worried because he had heard that without visas we would only be allowed to stay 48 hours. There was no cause for alarm: we cleared and got our visas with no problem.

When I got ashore, I thought, what a change from Mexico. The island itself is a lush and tropical green. Everyone I met along the road smiled and said "Bonjour." The people have such a pleasant and friendly air about them. The contrast between Mexicans and Polynesians is amazing. Before the day was over we were loaded with bananas, papayas, limes, and coconuts that various people gave us.

One of the more interesting of our new friends was Hina. She speaks French, Polynesian, and a little English. When we met her, she said, "You come see me, no bullshit." There is a story of how Hina came to live in Taiohae. I don't know if it is true, but I'll pass it on anyway. Her family and home is on another island in the Marquesas, where a yacht stopped on its way to Tahiti. It seems that it is the life ambition of all the islanders of French Polynesia to go one day to Papeete in Tahiti. Hina was no exception and she was able to get free passage on the yacht. The yacht had to stop at Nuku Hiva to get permission from the governor before Hina could go to Papeete. But the governor would not give his permission, so Hina had to get off the yacht in Taiohea. As she had no means of support and no way to return to her home island, the governor let her work in his house. It seems Hina was caught stealing some trifle from the Governor's house and put in the local jail. In the same jail was Joe, also there for some small matter. In the natural course of events, Hina became pregnant, so she and Joe were let out of jail to start a family. Now they have three lovely children.

One evening the local people had a luau for us on the beach. The table was huge banana leaves placed on the sand. The dishes were half-coconut shells and the silverware, our fingers. There was food laid out before us I had read about but never really believed to exist or that I would ever eat. There was kalua pig, roast chicken, breadfruit, poi, and some strange vegetables. I had heard a lot about the poi of the South Seas but wasn't impressed by it. It's rather hard to describe the taste, since there wasn't much taste to it. I sat there after the meal on the beach listening to the music and watching the wild Marquesan dancing, asking myself over and over again whether this was a dream.

There was another luau before we left Nuku Hiva, this one in honor of Joe's birthday. I dug around in the boat, looking for a gift for him and found a bright red shirt. But the next day it was Hina who was parading around in the shirt. There are many sports on the island but the one I enjoyed the most watching was the town baker giving people water-ski rides behind his outboard boat. It was obvious it was a new sport and they were just learning. The baker came by our boat one afternoon and asked if any of us would like to try and ski. Naturally we all said yes and I got out my slalom ski from the lazaret. Sue was in the water first and made a perfect deep-water start. The baker pulled her all around the bay, before dropping her off at the beach. The whole town was there watching and they all looked that single ski over. It seems they had never heard of a slalom ski before. The outcome was that the islanders spent the next week trying to master the slalom. The governor also had a try one evening. Two boys finally mastered it but the doctor's wife, Titi, tried up to the day we left, but could never make it. Titi is a picture-postcard of a Polynesian girl: tall, slim, long black hair, and very beautiful. She comes from the island of Hiva Oa and is quite a contrast to the girls here who are very big, with huge feet. They are not particularly attractive.

August 12—We raised anchor and departed Taiohae Bay at 09:30. We aren't leaving because we are tired of this paradise but because it is such a fabulous place we want to hurry on and discover more wonderful ports. The town's

Manihi Atoll

The young women of Manihi weren't just smiling for the camera, they smiled all the time. They were very affectionate (notice that they have their arms around each other). And they seem very happy, though they live their entire lives on the small coral atoll and dream of sailing to Papeete, the center of their world. In the photo, the women with Suttie are, from the left, Toumato, Toana, and Marguerita.

people turned out to wish us "Bon Voyage." Tia brought each of us a lei. It was sad leaving such truly friendly people. They weren't wonderful because of the parties or all the fresh fruit they gave us, but because they gave of themselves. They were most gracious. Two Marquesan words stick in my mind: kanahau (good) and kaikai (food). We were headed for Manihi Atoll in the Tuamotu Archipelago, also called the Dangerous Islands. The next four days was what I had pictured South Sea cruising to be: calm seas, light breezes, and warm sunshine.

August 16—For some reason we sighted Takaroa rather than Manihi (the navigators wouldn't tell me how that happened), and made for Takaroa. We entered the pass from the west, with the setting sun reflecting off the surface of the water, and tied up to the quay at 18:45. The log read 460 miles. The next morning, when we could see the pass through the reef more clearly, we got sick to our stomachs because we saw that we could have easily missed the channel and ended up on the reef. In bright day light it can be clearly seen. We pushed our luck this time but never again will we come through a reef without good visibility. The people were on the quay to greet us and we invited them aboard. Before long the musical instruments were out and everyone was singing. Music is always a good way to communicate when there is a language barrier. My background of French from my mother has been a big help. John Parker, who works for the government as a weatherman on the island, speaks a little English and was telling us the names of some of the people. Many were named after movie stars: Eleanor Parker, Robert Taylor, Errol Flynn, Bettie Davis, and so forth.

The next morning he came over to tell us we shouldn't let all these people on board at the same time, just one at a time. He said most of these people had been sent over from Tahiti because of some crime they had committed or because they were undesirables. It seems that this atoll is some kind of penal colony.

August 19—We left Takaroa yesterday and arrived at Manihi today at 12:00. The log read 62 miles. After just an hour here I can see a big contrast between Takaroa and Manihi. Manihi is clean looking and the people look happy, pleasant, and contented. On our arrival the people all came aboard, but wouldn't go below deck, unless invited. Madame Tuxana came aboard and invited Adel and me to take a bath at her house. This was very much appreciated, more so when we found out how scarce the water is on the atoll. Madam Tuxana invited all of us over for dinner, then again for lunch and dinner the next day.

The younger people start coming aboard during breakfast and stay until midnight. The bigger boys ask to play our musical instruments and sit in the stern of the schooner making music all day. If they stop, the girls pick up the instruments and play. They are very polite people and as I've said, will not go below unless invited. But they will, from the youngest to the oldest, stick their heads down the skylights and watch everything going on below deck. They watch Adel cooking and us eating. We had to put a cover over the skylight in the head. It's a little embarrassing to be sitting on the head, and then look up and see smiling faces peering down. Even with the cover on, they tended to lift it up and peer down—until I explained to them we did not appreciate it. From then on, the only privacy we had was in the head.

There are three religions on the island: Catholic, Mormon, and Sanito. The majority of the people belong to the Sanito Church, which is related to the Mormon Church. Unlike the Catholics, the Mormons and Sanitos are forbidden to smoke, drink, and dance. After marriage dancing is allowed. There are two occupations on the atoll: diving for pearls and cutting copra. One of the leading citizens is a pearl diver who could dive to 27 meters. He is retired now because of the bends. At the present, the atoll is in between the pearl season and the copra season, so people have time on their hands, particularly the young adults. They are called on to play basketball, volleyball, or what they call football every afternoon. The unmarried girls usually play against the married women. It seems that each island throughout Polynesia has a Chinese family that owns the local store. I have yet to see a store owned by a Polynesian. Each home has its own garden plot made from soil that has been brought in from Tahiti.

For some reason all the girls like Jon. So I sold him for five francs to Marguerita Nicolai, whose mother is the chief. Louise bought Verne and Toumato bought Rick. I even sold Pat to Amillion. That made Pat happy to think he had a girl too. They all think Pat is pretty because of his blonde hair, blue eyes, and fair skin. One of the girls, Toana, dances the tamure and gets Jon to dance with her (she's Catholic). Only thing is, Jon can't tamure, but he does some step that gets the people howling with laughter and begging for more. I wanted to get pictures of these wonderful people but was afraid at first for fear they would not

Papeete

In 1962 Papeete was little more than a village. Tahiti had plenty of fresh water, and the crew washed their clothes and took showers on the sea wall along Boulevard Pomare. In the photo, Suttie is doing her laundry with Fairweather *in the background, tied stern-to and with her awnings rigged.*

like being photographed. I finally got my camera out and asked if I could take their picture. They were very pleased to pose for me, and in fact they all wanted to have their picture taken.

One afternoon the boys went spear fishing with some of the island men in the lagoon. All they managed to catch was a huge eel. That evening Madam Tuxana sent over a bowl of the cooked eel. I was all for tasting some and offered some to our many guests who were on board. They wouldn't eat any, so I decided not to try it. Our guests preferred peanut butter and jam on crackers. We went through four jars of peanut butter in two days.

All the girls told me the whole town will cry when we leave. When we did leave it was in such a hurry that there was no time for tears. I'm glad it was that way because there would have been a few tears shed on the boat as well. We have a new crew member, Tiriki, one of the boys of the atoll. The village people think it's a wonderful chance for him to see the world and, as they have hinted, maybe to find a nice fat wife. He will be our cook when Adel leaves us in Tahiti.

August 25—We left Manihi for Rangiroa at 11:00. Rangiroa is only a hundred miles to the southwest, but we were slowed by strong winds, and had to continue under storm-trysail. We reached the pass at Rangiroa just after sunset the next day, and remembering Takaroa, we hove-to for the night. There were gale force winds all night, and the next morning we discovered that the storm had blown us far down wind. Since we couldn't beat our way back to the pass against the winds and high seas, we set our course for Tahiti. Poor Tiriki is seasick. We are sailing under jib and storm-trysail and making seven knots.

August 29—We sighted Tahiti at sunrise. The pilot boat came out and led us through the pass. We moored stern to the quay in front of the town at 11:00. The log read 300 miles. First thing the other yachts asked us when we arrived was about the weather outside. They had heard it was a full gale and that two sailboats from Tahiti had been lost. I knew we had been through a storm but no worse than what we had crossing the Pacific. Everything below was completely soaked. Drying out came later. First we had to have a Hinano, the famous Tahitian beer.

In the evening, while walking past Quinn's Bar, I saw Verne come out through the swinging doors. His eyes just glowed with the knowledge that he was really in Tahiti. Later that night, Verne saw Tiriki sitting on the boat in his only pair of shorts. So Verne started hauling out his clothes and giving them to Tiriki: sport coats, white shirts, slacks, suits, ties, and one pair of boxer shorts. I know when Verne sobers up in a day or two he will wish he hadn't been so generous.

Adel left the boat in the morning. I hated to see her go but the Captain said she had to. She was an interesting person. I asked Tiriki to come shopping with me to break him in as cook. Since this was his first time away from the small atoll of Manihi, he wanted to dress up in his new clothes. When he came up on deck I couldn't say a word—he had such a happy grin on his face. He had put on one of Verne's white shirts with a tie and those boxer shorts. So that's the way we went shopping. In the evening he went to the movies in a sport coat and the boxer shorts. No one had the heart to tell him that his clothes were not as fashionable as he seemed to think.

I've been trying to teach Tiriki to cook. He doesn't speak a word of English and he doesn't understand my French. (I finally found out that he doesn't speak French either.) Everything I say to him he replies with, "Oui, Mama." I now use the system of showing him pictures of what to prepare for the meals. Bill rented a car for a few days. Tiriki gets up with the sun, washes and polishes the car, then sits behind the wheel the rest of the day. Then he disappeared for three days. When he returned he was all smiles and kissing everyone like he was so happy to be back. A week later he disappeared for another few days. It was impossible to find out where he went. We still haven't found a way of communicating with him. Then one day he disappeared for good. I guess he must have found the big fat wife he was looking for. He never did learn to cook, although he snorted and grunted long and loud in the galley trying.

With the help of seventy-year-old John Nash, an Englishman trying to get permanent residence in Tahiti, I was able to get Sue and Pat into the Catholic school. Only French is spoken in the school and Pat is very unhappy, but Sue enjoys it and is doing well. School is from seven to eleven in the morning, and then again after lunch, from two to five.

Two American yachts have come in. One is the *Nordleys*, with two families and eight children on board. The other is the *Nimbus*, a forty-foot ketch with six people and four bunks. They really had Papeete agape the day they landed, as they fought with each other from one end of town to the other.

Bora Bora

The silhouette of Bora Bora is a well-known image of French Polynesia. In the photo, Fairweather *is approaching the island, and in the lower part of the photo, the taffrail of the schooner ends at the main shrouds. The motor bike lashed to the shrouds made it as far as Fiji before succumbing to salt water.*

We transferred Adel off our papers and onto the 110-foot schooner, *Dwen Wynn*. She was the talk of the town for a while. She spent one night in jail for tearing up a hotel room. The jail time seemed to calm her down because she has behaved herself ever since. As Maurice, the gendarme, said "Adel and the *Dwen Wynn* deserve each other." The entire crew of the *Dwen Wynn* left the schooner in Papeete, except the Captain and First Mate.

The Captain of the *Nimbus* reminds me of a character out of Henry Morgan, with his red beard and huge frame. He has picked up the worst of the Quinn girls and they are all living with him on his boat. Everyone else has moved off. He must take care of them all and make them happy because they cook for him, wash for him, and clean the boat for him.

October 30—After two months in Tahiti, we sailed to Moorea at 10:00. We have a new crew member, Raymond Pettigrove, an Australian who will be doing the cooking for us. When we reached Moorea, we anchored next to the *Wanderer* in Papetoai Bay, with our stern tied to coconut trees. The log read 15 miles. I thought Tahiti was beautiful, but Moorea is more so. We had dinner aboard the *Wanderer* with Captain Darr and his wife. The next morning the boys went hunting for wild pig and after two hours they were back with one that Rick shot. The Tahitian boys cleaned it, and then buried it over hot rocks with some breadfruit and bananas. That was one delicious meal. The pork had a wild flavor. After Tahiti, Moorea is so quiet and peaceful. The *Wanderer* supplied us with three bunches of bananas and a box of avocados. Verne and Rick's girlfriends came over from Papeete to meet them here, and they gave us pineapples and papayas, so now we have plenty of fruit for our passage to Huahine. Rick's girlfriend also gave him ten pareos, a shirt, and a bathing suit.

November 2—We left Moorea at 11:00 and sailed for Huahine, seventy miles to the west. Rick set the course and Bill estimated the time when we would sight the island, but his estimate was not to Huahine but to Raiatea, which is ninety miles away. Verne was on watch at three in the morning and saw what he thought was a big black cloud up ahead. He knew it couldn't be Huahine, because we had gone only seventy miles and had twenty more to go. He called the Captain and the Captain called Rick. It was Huahine, and we tied up this morning at 09:00. The log read 90 miles.

November 4—We left Huahine this morning and sailed to Raiatea, arriving at 13:45. The log read 30 miles. Nothing but rain, rain, rain. But the sail over from Huahine was one of our best sails, with good winds and calm seas. I told Ray this morning I would do the cooking on the weekends and he could stand my watches while at sea. I don't want to frighten him off with all the cooking because he sure is a good cook. At least he cooks the way I like to eat, and he's fast.

November 7—We left Raiatea at 10:00 and sailed for Bora Bora, taking the pass through the reefs between Raiatea and Tahaa. Verne was up on the crosstrees, Rick was reading the chart, and the Captain was at the helm. We went through under main and genoa. We arrived in Bora Bora that afternoon at 15:00. The log read 30 miles. As soon as we were tied to the quay, the islanders came with their souvenirs. There were at least thirty people lay-ing out their wares on the shore. We explained to them that we no longer had any Tahitian money. Someone asked if we had any pants and shirts to trade. Of course, we had all kinds of old clothes to trade. I really think that they got the better of the deal, but everyone was happy. Even Sue and Pat got into the act and traded the clothes they had outgrown. While I was over having a cold beer, Pat traded all his clothes except what he was wearing. And what did we get? Souvenirs that all together we could have bought for five dollars. I would love to see the men who got Verne's wool suits wearing them in this heat.

November 9—We didn't leave Bora Bora today as planned. Wednesday afternoon we all went out to look at the naval installations that the Americans built during the war. Along the old navy dock, yachts had painted their names and the dates they were here. I asked Verne to paint *Fairweather*, but it takes him so long to do anything that we were gone before he decided to start. Maybe it's a good thing he didn't start, since we did leave the name of *Fairweather* on everyone's lips. We went through some of the old navy huts where books, drugs, and ammunition had been left. The boys picked up a few bullets for souvenirs and then we stopped for a few beers, before returning to the boat for dinner. It was after dinner that the gendarmes came. Bill hadn't brought the papers to the gendarmes to clear, so he thought this was what they wanted and he went with them with our passports. After fifteen minutes of talking through an interpreter, he found out that we were accused of trespassing and stealing a box of ammunition. He admitted that we had looked through the old navy installation, but that we hadn't taken anything. When he got

Samoa

Many of the houses in Samoa were still very traditional. As Suttie describes them in her journal, "the homes are oval in shape with thatch roofs that are held up with poles about four feet apart. The floor is ground coral. And so there is just one room that is completely open. The people use woven mats to sit on and sleep on."

back to the boat, he told the boys to get rid of the ammunition, so they took it out in the dingy and sank it in the lagoon. We couldn't leave the next morning because the gendarmes had our passports and they wouldn't give them back until we gave the ammunition back—which was now impossible. The Polynesians were doing the accusing and the gendarmes were in the middle. We were also accused of spying, but I don't know who we were spying on or for. The talk that's going around is that there was a group of rebel Polynesians who are planning a revolt to throw out the French. It was a tense situation. The French didn't want the ammunition returned, but they felt that they had to appease the Polynesians. After talking all day Thursday, we realized that they could keep us here indefinitely. So Rick became our scapegoat. He told them where the ammunition was. (I want to say here that the really guilty person was our Captain: he told Rick and Jon to go back at night and steal a box of ammunition.) The gendarmes wrote up a report that was favorable to Rick. He had to fly over to Raiatea the next day and report to the judge. That made Jon unhappy that he didn't volunteer as the scapegoat because he missed out on the airplane ride. We brought the boat back to Raiatea on Friday, and on Saturday morning Rick and the Captain went before the judge. The judge scared them at first by telling them they could be sent to jail from one to five years and fined a million francs. But he let Rick off with an eight dollar fine and no jail term. But he had to wear a special green shirt all day. After we all had a beer to celebrate, we left for Pago Pago at 15:00. Between Raiatea and Bora Bora we saw the *Nordleys* making for the Bora

Bora pass, and we wondered what kind of reception they would get after the mess we had left.

November 11—Now this is the kind of sailing I enjoy—all sails set in smooth seas and warm, moderate winds. The Captain figures that at the most it will take us ten days to reach Pago Pago.

November 13—A squall hit during my watch, while the crew was below serenely eating dinner. I could hear them talking but they couldn't hear me screaming for help. The wind was howling, and I couldn't see because of the rain. I was using both hands, trying to keep the boat from broaching-to in the following sea. One wave caught us abeam and laid the boat over on her side—water everywhere. I couldn't raise anybody from below. I thought the last wave would get someone up, but after the first five minutes of being frightened, I began to enjoy the fury of the wind and seas. About half an hour later Rick came up and, when he saw the wind and sea, he yelled below, "On deck." We lowered all the sails but the foresail, and we were still doing seven knots.

November 16—Ray made bread today. The first batch went over the side. The second batch came out fine. Sue and Pat have fallen behind in their school work. They started studying Monday and can't seem to get their minds to concentrate. Now I have them studying all day. I help them in the mornings and in the afternoons they must read, make an outline of what they have read, and write a composition from their outline. The compositions are getting better each day. At least they are able to concentrate more.

November 19—We tied to the quarantine buoy in Pago Pago Harbor at 23:45. The log read 1149 miles. We have managed to make another port at night. After clearing in the morning, we went ashore to find all the islanders speaking English with an American accent. I don't know why I should be so surprised, since the island has been under American control since before 1900.

The Samoans are very kind, but the island seems to suffer from American subsidies. Food is not cheap. Fresh vegetables are not to be found. The few pineapples, bananas, and papayas are very expensive. Eggs are $1.25 a dozen—when they are available. There are no facilities for yachts such as showers or fresh water. There's not even a dock to tie up to. Even so we were charged nine dollars a week for staying there.

Wednesday night the Port Captain invited us to his club house, the Goat Island Club. It was pleasant talking to Americans. When the club closed, Bill and I went over to the radio operator's house (Williams was his name) for more refreshments. When we left to call for our dinghy, no one on board heard us, so Williams invited us to spend the night at his house. Everything was fine until later that night when a slight noise woke me up. I could see a dim form coming into the bedroom, take off its clothes and get into bed next to me. I felt with my hand on the other side of me and there was Bill. Then some hands began to paw me. I climbed over on the other side of Bill and finally shook him awake. Then I turned on the light and saw Williams in bed with us with a rather silly look on his face. He was all apologetic the next morning. I am still wondering about that strange event. Maybe this is what goes on in the islands. Bill didn't seem to mind but I wasn't cut out for that kind of stuff.

Sue, Pat, and I took a bus ride into the back country. After reading the history of Samoa and its people, I wanted to see more of the island. The homes are oval in shape with thatch roofs that are held up with poles about four feet apart. The floor is ground coral. And so there is just one room that is completely open. The people use woven mats to sit on and sleep on. Tattooing is still practiced among the men but not as much as before. They are generally tattooed from the waist to the knees.

The generator burnt up—Jon has been accused of not putting oil in it—so we are here for longer than expected. We moved the boat over to the dry dock next to the Japanese fishing fleet. The Japanese fishermen turned out to be very good company. The head cook made us a typical Japanese lunch—rice balls wrapped in seaweed with raw fish. The generator is finally fixed, so now we can leave. The *Nordleys* has come and gone. We are to meet them in Suva, Fiji.

December 2—Everything was ship-shape as we left Pago Pago and sailed for Suva at 09:00. We couldn't find the navigation plotter, but we had an extra one.

December 3—We can still see Tutuila (American Samoa) astern. No wind and it's hot. Sue and Pat wanted to go swimming, so we lowered the boarding ladder over the side. Just as Pat was ready to jump in, Ray sighted a fin cutting through the water. Then we saw three sharks circling the boat. That put an end to the idea of swimming over the side. Ray baited a hook with tinned meat wrapped in gauze. It was fascinating watching the sharks make passes at the bait, hitting it with the sides of their bodies. Then from a distance we could see the largest shark come straight for the bait and take it. He put up no fight but came straight to the boat. We had more sense than to bring a live shark on board, so we cut the line above the hook.

December 4—Still no wind. We are drifting slowly back to Samoa. We have three hundred miles of diesel and we will need most of it to get through the reefs of the Fiji Islands. After some thought the Captain decided to power for two hundred miles in the hope of finding some wind.

December 5—We had to turn off the engine to save fuel but then a breeze came up. Now we are under full sail, making four knots.

December 11—We lost a day crossing the International Date Line, but we pick up a fair wind and sailed into Suva and dropped anchor at noon. The log read 689 miles. This was one of the few occasions when we arrived at a port in the daytime. The *Nordleys* has been here for three days.

I was very impressed with the Fijian people when we went into town. They are fine looking people. From the head alone, it is difficult to tell a man from a woman. Both sexes have the same big, bushy hair. The people seem to be very proud of their hair and take good care of it. I was not impressed with the Indians in Suva. The women, as a rule, are beautiful and dress in attractive saris, but unlike the Fijians, they are not very friendly. We spent Christmas here and it was not like Christmas in the States. Here, Christmas is more of a holiday for the adults than for the children. In town all the plate glass store windows are boarded up on Christmas Eve because of the Fijians and their merry making. The Indians keep to themselves.

The Royal Suva Yacht Club is a relaxing and pleasant place for a cold beer and steak sandwich. The New Zealanders here have made us feel very welcome. To show our appreciation we had a barbecue on the boat one evening and invited all the people who were so kind to us. Rick, Verne, and Ray went to the Yacht Club last night. Ray was standing at the bar drinking a beer, with his change on the bar in front of him. A South African came up to the bar next to Ray and ordered a drink and paid for it out of Ray's change. Ray asked him what the hell he thought he was doing with his money, and the South African told Ray he was crazy, that the money on the bar was his. Ray called him a dirty son-of-a-bitch or some such thing, and so the South African knocked him down. Ray got up and proceeded to beat the living daylights out of him. Rick was sitting on a bar stool rooting for Ray when Larry from the *Nordleys* knocked Rick off his stool. That upset Verne, so he jumps on Larry's back. It turned into quite a free-for-all. Ray was finally subdued with his arms held down when the Secretary of the Club came up to Ray and hit him. Ray broke loose and flattened the Secretary. The little Chinese cook was running around with a meat cleaver and threatened to cut up anyone who hit Ray again.

   The next morning at eight o'clock the Secretary came to the boat with a letter saying that the *Fairweather* and her crew were no longer welcome at the Yacht Club. This was a little upsetting for Bill. He thought he deserved a hearing before being expelled from the Yacht Club. When Don Nickleson of the Royal New Zealand Air Force heard about it, things began to happen. Don made an appointment with the Commodore of the Yacht Club in the afternoon. Don, Bill, Ray, and the other fellows involved were there. When all the facts from both sides were heard, the *Fairweather* was reinstated in the Yacht Club and the South African who started it all was blackballed. But Ray was blackballed too.

Don made arrangements with one of the Fijians under his command to let us visit his village and watch some dancing and kava drinking. Bill didn't see anything interesting in that and refused to go. Ray came and it turned out to be a fascinating day. To me, one of the purposes of this cruise was to see how other people in the world live. In most of the islands we have stopped at, I have been fortunate to meet people of the island and be invited into their homes. Anyway, before the dancing began, a kava ceremony was performed. As the kava is presented to each person in turn, the natives clap their hands. It is thought rude not to drink the kava, which is served in a half coconut shell. After everything that I had heard about kava, I expected it to taste pretty horrible, but it was rather refreshing. I was told that many years ago the kava root was chewed by virgins and the juice spat into a container. Now it is made more hygienically. I was not impressed by their dancing. I expected a rather wild type of dancing to fit with the image of the "wild" Fijian. The women do their dancing in a sitting position and just move their hands in time to the music.

Three weeks have gone by and it is getting later into the hurricane season, so we must be moving down south to New Zealand. Everyone says we have been very lucky with the weather in Suva. It has been excellent with just a little rain and I can believe that after all I've read about the rains of Fiji. The *Nordleys* won't be ready to leave for another week, so we will meet them in New Zealand.

January 3, 1962—We left Suva at 17:00 and set sail for Russell, New Zealand, 1,000 miles to the south.

January 7—Ray woke up feeling good this morning. He gets so sea sick when we start a passage in rough weather. And it has been rough. No storms, just good strong winds. We are heeling over so far that the lee rail is often in the water and we are taking a lot of it on deck. It's wet but we are making good time. On this point of sail, with the wind just forward of the beam, *Fairweather* steers herself. The weather is getting cooler and cooler as we sail farther south. During the night watches we are wearing jackets and shoes now. Sue and Pat are very susceptible to tropical sores. I hope this cooler weather will clear them up.

January 9—The Royal New Zealand Air Force from Suva flew over and circled a few times, then turned back toward Suva. It's nice to have friends.

January 10—We sighted New Zealand this morning. In the distance it looks rather bleak and desolate. A yacht, the *Atea*, came out to meet us and show us where to tie up. That was the first time someone met us. But I have found the New Zealanders exceptional. We tied to the pier at 15:00. The log read 1020 miles. As soon as the boat was secured, people started coming aboard, bringing beer. Quite a party was going until a policeman came by and chased everyone off. We hadn't been cleared by the doctor yet. Russell is a resort town and this time of year is the southern summer and vacation time. Everyone takes off at least two weeks over the Christmas holidays and numerous businesses are closed. Boy, can these Kiwis drink beer. The pubs close at 18:00 and remain closed all day Sunday, but the Kiwis still have their beer. The hotel pub stays open

South Seas

until all hours and as a guest of the hotel, the pub is open. The women drink what they call a shanty, which is beer mixed with lemonade. I can't understand why they do that.

We went sailing with Dick and Pat McElvay across the bay and then went touring by car inland. We saw the forest of Kirie trees. The wood is known to make the best boats. There were fruit stands along the side of the road with no one tending them. The prices are all marked and there is usually a cigar box to leave money in. Anyone who wants to buy something helps himself. It seems to be an honor system that everyone accepts. But this is the only place so far that we had anything stolen. Someone pinched our ensign. They must have taken it as a joke but they haven't returned it yet. We met an American couple, Bob and Mary Kettridge, aboard their yacht *Svay*. They are sailing around the world.

Becalmed

Sailing from Auckland to Nouméa, Fairweather *was becalmed south of Norfolk Island for three days. The crew took the sails down, went for a swim, and waited, as the barometer began to drop and a typhoon approached from the northwest.*

East Indies

January 17—We powered all the way to Auckland. No wind and no charts. Powered all night and came into Auckland Harbor in the morning. No pilot met us, and as we heard that yachts can tie up to the pier at the old ferry building, that is where we tied up at 13:00. The log read 120 miles. The ferry building is at the end of Queens Street, which is the center of the city. And here we stayed for five months, right in the middle of everything. Being in the center of town has its advantages and disadvantages. There are always people on the pier looking at the boat. We have met many friends because of that. One day while I was in the stern cabin, I heard two men discussing the boat and where she was from. The *Fairweather* is registered in Georgetown, Grand Cayman, and on her stern, beneath her name, are the initials "G. C." But these two men, knowing we were Americans, thought that "G. C." stood for "Grand Canyon." They were trying to figure out how we got this boat down through the Grand Canyon and if there was a port there. After ten minutes of listening to them, I had to go on deck and tell them the letters stood for "Grand Cayman."

Being in town, shopping is not much of a chore, except different items are sold in different stores: bread in one, meat in another, fruit and vegetables in another, milk in

Auckland

Fairweather *spent five months moored to the ferry building at the end of Queen Street in Auckland, New Zealand. Here is where a major change took place on board, as Bill left the schooner and Suttie took his place as captain. In the photo, the center-cockpit ketch,* Marinero, *is moored alongside* Fairweather. *The* Marinero *lost a crew member overboard during the same typhoon that hit Fairweather off Norfolk Island.*

another, and so on. The supermarket has not arrived in Auckland yet. The food is of the highest quality and very reasonable. Everything that is manufactured or imported is expensive, compared to US prices. Wages are lower than in the US and taxes are high. To offset this, the people have a good pension, free medical, unemployment insurance, and child compensation. Everyone is taken care of.

We took the boat over to West Haven and went up on the grids. We tied the boat up to the pilings and when the tide went out, the boat was sitting on her keel in the mud. The boys got the bottom cleaned and painted before the tide came back in. We found a few worm holes, so we will go up on the ways at the end of the month to have them taken care of.

Received a letter from Sonya Holland and read the sad news that Fred Wittle and the *Karana* were lost during a hurricane off the Mexican coast between Zihuatanejo and Acapulco. Fred had taken Pearl back to the US by plane, so she wasn't aboard.

February 1—Bill went back to the States. The situation on the *Fairweather* has reached the point where something has to give. He will be gone for about two months. I hope he finds what he is looking for and realizes it's not worth it. Now the rest of us can relax and enjoy New Zealand.

The Royal Akarana Yacht Club had a reception for all the visiting yachtsmen. The skippers were asked to take a bow on stage, so I did the honors for *Fairweather*. Many other cruising yachtsmen were there as well. Bob and Mary Kettridge were there, plus the DeKonings on the *Nordleys,* Floyd and Doris Christensen on the *Marinero,* Kurt Asford on the *Sea Wife,* Bob and Nancy Griffith on

Asleep on Deck

The photo shows the deck of Fairweather *from the foremast looking aft. The boxes between the masts were for storing fresh fruit and vegetables. The barrels below them held kerosine for the galley stove. On top of the boxes is a reveler who is still asleep the morning after Ray's goodbye party.*

the *Awhanee,* and Norman Young on the *Diana.* Captain Young, as he is usually called, is in his seventies and on his seventh circumnavigation.

February 3—Ray is flying back to Australia, so a party was in order and it turned out to be one of the best on the *Fairweather*. As the people came on board, they were handed a pareo to put on. This started the party off in a relaxed mood.

I should explain about getting on and off *Fairweather*. With Auckland's twelve foot tide, it is quite a jump from the pier to the deck at low tide, so we tied a line from the topmast to the pier. To get on or off the boat, you just grab the line and swing across. We lost two girls during the party because they swung clear across the boat and landed on the other side, in the water. At the peak of the party, pareos were slipping down and out would pop a boob or two, but who cared. It was a great party to remember and Ray just made it to the airport the next morning.

February 5—Rick, Jon, and Verne started working on the wharfs. They must be there by seven to hand in their cards, and if there is work, they start at eight. It isn't steady work, so they have been able to work on the boat too. Sue and Pat have started going to school and love it. They ride the ferry across the bay to Davenport, so they miss all the traffic in town. The Captain of the ferry lets Pat take the helm in the morning. They have swimming at school and free milk. It's just great. They have also joined the swimming club at the Tysid Baths. At the first race Pat took a first in his class and Sue took a second in hers.

And that leaves me all day on the boat by myself, but I haven't been lonesome. Who could be lonesome in New

Zealand? Everyone is so friendly and I mean really friendly. I've sailed on different boats, visited Rotorua, and seen the glow worms. The more I see of this country, the more I like it. With Bill gone, it has been like a pleasant and relaxing vacation.

April 4—Bill came back today. Melanie Janus, Rick's girlfriend from California, arrived with him. I don't know why he came back. He is worse than ever. His latest actions while sailing during the Easter week has caused a complete break in our relationship. It is either he leaves the boat or I leave. Rick and Jon have begged me not to go, so he is leaving. That was his choice anyway. He prefers having no responsibilities. It is strange what a little money and power can do to a man who has never had either before.

As for money, he has promised us $500 per month and we can do as we wish. I have three possibilities. One, stay here in New Zealand with the children and build a future. Two, sail back to the States—and admit defeat. Or three, continue on with the world cruise. After much thought, the obvious course is to continue the cruise, and after talking it over with my boys, they are behind me all the way. So now the *Fairweather* has a new captain—me. I have always felt there wasn't anything I couldn't do and now I have the chance to prove it. I did fail in my marriage of eighteen years, but sometimes the forces are too great to fight. I feel bad about the children no longer having a father, especially Sue and Pat, but some fathers are worse than none, as Bill has shown. Do I feel bad about the separation personally? Yes, in a way. He has been a part of me for so many years and I have come to depend on him, but I know when this vague feeling disappears, it will be the best thing that has ever happened to me—and the children. I will be free mentally to think and feel and say as I want, as everyone has a right to expect.

Now to the business of taking command of the boat and her crew. I wired Ray in Australia, saying that we were leaving in a week, and if he wanted to join us, his bunk was ready. He arrived two days later. As for provisioning, that was always my job, so there was no problem there. I also put on board fifteen cases of beer, two cases of gin, one of scotch and one of rum. It sounds like we are heavy drinkers, but that isn't true. I'm going to have a cocktail hour at sea. Between 16:00 and 17:00 we can all sit around the helm with a drink and shoot the breeze. Also, I want some spirits on board so that in the different ports we are able to entertain the people we meet. I want this boat to be a happy one. I want everyone to feel the *Fairweather* is their home as well as mine and to treat her as such. Something was wrong about the feeling and personality of the boat before now and I hope to change that.

I had to plan our cruise, especially where to be at certain times of year, in order to take advantage of good weather and avoid bad weather. I didn't want to go to Hong Kong and Japan, as originally planned, and after looking over the wind charts and doing some reading, I decided to go to Singapore by way of New Caledonia, New Hebrides, Port Moresby, Torres Straits, Darwin, Bali, and Java. In Singapore I will plan the next leg. As close as I can figure, we will reach Singapore sometime in November.

May 21—I didn't know the first thing about getting clearance from the port, although I knew it had to be done, but it didn't take me long to learn, and at 12:30 we slipped the lines and powered out of Auckland harbor. There was no charge for using the ferry wharf for the past five months. All the friends we met in New Zealand were there to wish us "Bon Voyage" and good luck.

On board as we set sail were my four children, Rick, Jon, Sue and Pat; Verne Hansen, who has been with us since San Francisco; Raymond Pettigrove from Australia; Mel Janus; Harold Stephens, who sailed from Tahiti on the *Nordleys* and who wanted to go to Nouméa with us; and myself. I wish I could say I set the course for Nouméa, but Rick does the navigating. Eventually I want to learn and have at least the satisfaction of knowing how.

May 23—It has rained for the past two days. Last night we were under foresail and still logging seven knots, until the sail ripped from leech to luff. This is the first time that Mel has done any sailing and she is beginning to think we are all crazy, if this is a sample of what it is like. Ray stepped on a piece of glass the day before we left port and had to have some stitches. Today he not only is still seasick, but his foot has become infected. Every time I give him a penicillin pill, he vomits it up. Steve said he would give him a penicillin shot if he doesn't improve in the next few hours.

I came on deck this morning to a beautiful, warm day with a light breeze. It's like stepping from one world into the next overnight. We had our first cocktail hour and enjoyed the South Sea cruising.

May 28—We have spent the last four days drifting in flat, calm weather. No one seems to mind. Everyone is relaxed and enjoying himself swimming, having a beer, and listening to the music. We put our daily ration of beer in a gunny afraid of death but felt sorry that I had brought everyone else on board into this. I thought of that storm as a test of strength and endurance for the boat, the crew, and myself. The *Fairweather* came through like any well-built boat. The crew was well satisfied that they were able to handle such a storm. And I knew from now on that nothing could stop us. The next three days were squally and miserable but we were able to sail under reefed sails, averaging seven knots.

June 3—We sighted New Caledonia at noon. Some of the plans everyone was making for when they got ashore sounded pretty wild. Everyone sounds so happy, satisfied, and pleased with our present situation that I am satisfied as well.

June 4—Since I didn't want to go in through the pass in the barrier reef at night, we hove-to until morning, then sailed into Nouméa harbor and tied up to the wharf at 12:30. The log read 1205 miles. We were fourteen days at sea.

Mr. Hubbard (Bebe), head of the yacht club, met us and became our interpreter and took care of all the paper work for me. All of the officials were surprised that *Fairweather* had a woman skipper. Bebe took us to the bank and post office (you have to have your passport to get your mail) and showed us the town. We brought the boat around to Fishermen's Bay and anchored out. Then we went to town. The meals are not too expensive, but beer is almost a dollar a bottle. We will be doing our drinking on board from now on. The town is quaint and French. Very little English is spoken. Verne passed out, as usual, and we had to carry him home.

Nouméa

Fairweather *moored at the yacht club's floating dock in Fishermen's Bay. The mooring was far from town but close to the island's beaches to the south. In the photo, Verne, who was born and raised in Hawaii, is carving a tiki head. The tiki was used for the bow of the outrigger that the crew built in Nouméa.*

I got a letter from Sid and he said there was quite a storm last Tuesday around Cape Britt, and New Zealand had some of the biggest seas they had ever seen. So that was quite a storm we were in.

June 5—I sent the kids to the store for eggs this morning. It turns out that they cost two dollars a dozen, so we won't be eating eggs while we are here.

June 22—In another two days we will have been here three weeks. Out of those three weeks we have had only one sunny day. It's been rainy, windy, and squally since we have been here. We are tied up to the floating dock at the Yacht Club Baie des Pecheurs (Fishermen's Bay) about three miles out of town.

Steve left two weeks ago for Australia and we all miss his happy smile and his "What a Life" attitude. I got a letter from him yesterday. He is getting the story of the *Fairweather* going through that storm, and Ray being the hero, printed in a local newspaper. He also mentioned the New Zealand woman on the *Svay* who was lost overboard on the way to Port Moresby. Also, the *Diana* was demasted outside of Sidney.

The people are so different in little ways the world over. Here in New Caledonia everybody seems to dislike everyone else. The French that have lived here all their lives don't like the French that come here from France on work contracts, and they call them frogs. They compare them to the Pommes in New Zealand. And of course they have nothing to do with the natives. The French that come here for short terms hate everything and everybody.

The Bar Ritz is our hang out. All the best people go there. Mel and I found us a bar in town we can go to after we do our shopping. Going to town is quite a challenge—to see how far we have to walk before we get a ride. So far we have had to do no walking. And getting back takes some thinking. If we catch a bus, we ask the bus driver to bring us down to our boat and they always have.

We were invited up to Group Commander H.M.S. Marshall Wright for drinks Tuesday night. What a big and beautiful house. Dennis Wright is an interpreter for the South Pacific Council and travels throughout the islands to study how the government can help the natives. The commander is quite a gay dog for his age—he looks 45 but he is 60. We had open house (open boat?) yesterday for all the yacht people. The Commodore invited only the best people, he said. Well just a few showed up and he was fit to be tied. He said he is resigning from the yacht club this morning. There may not have been very many people here but I think we all had a good time. Verne, Ray, Bebe, and I went to the Bar Ritz afterwards and closed the place down.

The boys have been building an out-rigger canoe. Verne has carved a tiki for the bow. They would have got it almost finished today, if it hadn't rained. Looks like I may have trouble with one of my crew and just the one I expected and the way I expected it, but she knew the rules when she joined the boat, so soon as we are alone I will tell her the facts as I see them. I like her but the morale of this boat will not be disrupted by her. I later explained the facts as I saw them to Mel and she has agreed to abide by the rules. Time will tell.

July 1—The Japanese fleet (four destroyers) was in port last week. This was the first Japanese visit to Nouméa since the war, so it was a big affair. They were having a party on board Thursday night for all the important people—by invitation only. Mel and I decided to go even though we had no invitation. We went down to the dock at 18:00 when it started. All of Nouméa was standing around watching the important people march down to the gangway, hand their invitation to a Japanese officer, and then being saluted as they boarded the ship. We realized we would never make it on board dressed the way we were, so we grabbed a taxi and rushed back to *Fairweather*, put our party clothes on in two minutes, and then rushed back to town. With our heads held high, we marched right up to gangway past the saluting officer and on to the ship. There were all kinds of Japanese food to eat and sake to drink. An officer invited us to his cabin for a party afterwards, but when we went looking for him later, we ended up in front of the admiral's cabin—with a guard in front who wouldn't let us in. So Mel stood there in front of the open door and winked and smiled at the admiral, who then came out and invited us to his private party. It was very dry and boring though, and after passing a few pleasantries with the mayor of Nouméa, we left for the Bar Ritz. It was an enjoyable evening.

July 8—We met the butcher, Morris. He took Jon, Ray, and me for a ride in his jeep around the country. We stopped at his friends in the bush and picked a gunny sack full of oranges. He stopped by today with deer and beef sausages. The boys haven't been able to finish their outrigger. They ran out of glue and have not been able to find any in Nouméa.

Ray found a can of mincemeat pie filling in a locker, so he made a pie for lunch. He added a can of roast beef to make more filling. Then he served it topped with catsup.

In New Zealand and Australia hamburger is called mincemeat. It didn't taste too bad but what a laugh we had. The boys now have the glue but the weather is too wet to finish their outrigger. Hope it clears up soon.

July 12—We have been playing poker, eating peanut butter sandwiches and drinking champagne, waiting for the storm that has been coming since last night. It's very calm and still, a prelude to a storm. As for the champagne we were drinking—Morris brought it over today, along with fish and huge prawns and cauliflower. Don't know why he brings all this food. Maybe he thinks we are poor. He even cooked the fish. Yesterday he gave me a ball the size of a bowling ball made of all the different hard woods of New Caledonia. Every day he brings something. It seems he remembers the Americans that were here during the war and they treated him well.

Looking on the dinner table last night we were amazed at the foods that come from different parts of the world. Mayonnaise from America, salt and pepper from New Zealand, Vegemite from Australia, wine from France, butter from Australia, bread from New Caledonia. It was quite interesting.

July 17—Our clearance was in order and we were ready to leave Nouméa. Morris brought over pork, veal, liver, and sausage—enough meat for a week. We left Nouméa at 17:00. The dock was crowded with people, some with tears in their eyes, waving good-bye as we left. The French warship *De Grasses* tapped us out. We wouldn't be able to make the Isle of Pines in one day, so we anchored that afternoon in Bonne Anse cove off Baie du Prony. The log read 16 miles.

July 18—We left the anchorage at 06:00 for Isle of Pines. After rounding the point of the bay, we found the wind blowing too strong to make any head way, so we returned to Bonne Anse. If we had kept on, night would have found us in the middle of those reef infested waters.

July 19—We got up at five and the wind was blowing stronger, so we went back to bed. Today we all got our skin-diving spears out and rowed around to a sandy beach, and when the tide went out on the reef, we went looking for octopus. We looked in holes in the reef for tentacles, and when we saw some, we put a little copper sulfate in the water. That made the octopus come rushing out. Then we grabbed it, turned it inside out, and beat it on the rocks. The boys caught six. We found bananas, coconuts, and papayas, and Ray speared two fish, so we had quite a meal. At the dinner table that night Mel said the smaller tentacles tasted better, but she called them "testicles," much to everyone's amusement. I can honestly say octopus is very good.

July 20—We sailed for Isle of Pines at 07:00. With all the meat on board we don't need any fish, but as it turned out, we caught two twenty-pound tuna. We arrived in Isle of Pine and anchored in Baie Kuto at 15:00. The log read 36 miles. Everyone was right: the Isle of Pine is beautiful. The sandy beaches are snow white and the water is crystal clear. We went to the hotel, took a hot shower and drank beer the rest of the afternoon. We sold the fish to the hotel for 600 francs and made reservations for dinner that night. So what did they serve us? The fish we had just sold them. And they charged us 1800 francs, plus 500 francs for a bottle of wine and three bottles of beer.

July 21—I hiked over to Vao village and saw the natives in their tree habitat. When the first white man visited the island, the natives were so taken by his white skin that whenever the natives visited the town, they would first go to the beach and rub the white sand all over their bodies, so they would look like the white men.

July 22—Raymond and Maurice, two vagabonds of the South Pacific, picked us up in their truck and showed us the island. Then we went to a small village where Raymond had made arrangements for a typical Melanesian feast. No one there spoke English but us, but we didn't need the spoken word to have a wonderful time. They roasted pig and fish, and then offered papaya and coffee. There was lots of beer and wine, and the rum I brought. And there was lots of singing and dancing. Later I invited them all over to the boat for a drink. It was the first time the natives saw the inside of a yacht, so it was quite a thrill for them.

July 23—The people at the hotel remarked that we must have had a good time last night because of all the noise we made. We got everything shipshape this morning and left for Port Villa in the New Hebrides at 10:00.

July 24—We were hove-to last night, with strong winds and high seas. Today we are making good progress under reefed main. We sighted the Loyalty Islands.

July 26—We anchored in Villa Harbor at 10:00. The log read 277 miles. The weather is beautiful. After being cleared by the customs, we anchored closer to Port Villa, cleaned up and went into town for the usual beer. It was good. Port Villa had nothing to offer in the way of entertainment. We spent one day exploring the beach with the dinghy and another day cleaning the boat inside and out.

The first two days were beautiful. After that it rained continually. Friday night, I should say Saturday morning at 02:00, Ray, Rick, Jon, and Verne came back with two huge lobsters, fresh bread, and the makings for a salad. So we had a big feast at 03:00. Things are a lot cheaper here than in Nouméa. A big stalk of bananas cost fifty cents. Eggs are still high. Paying for things is a little confusing. They add the bill up in French, I give them American dollars, and they give me change in British pounds and shillings.

A native tribe lives across the bay on an island and every morning and evening we can see their outriggers going to town and back. Most of the natives that live out of town have a tattoo of small dots high on one cheek. You can tell they are under the influence of the English because they keep in the background of the whites. If there is a group of natives waiting to buy something and a white person walks in, they all make way for him.

July 31—We left Port Villa at 10:00 for Luganville on Santos Island. The sky is overcast, but the wind is light, and we are on smooth starboard tack. This is the first time Mel has experienced good sailing since she joined us in New Zealand. She is still waiting for the tropical weather that she has heard so much about. We have a fishing line over as usual—may have some luck and catch a fish for dinner.

August 2—After five tries, we anchored in Luganville at 11:00. The log read 168 miles. We spent the rest of the day as usual in the bar—Carmen's Bar. She is a French woman in her early thirties who runs the most interesting bar.

August 3—Rick Powley and Denise Emirali off the yacht *Manu Moana* visited today. They are going up to Hong Kong and Japan. I spent the day up the river, and later saw

The Chart Table

The chart table was a drawer that pulled out. Suttie is actually standing at the chart table in the aft cabin, as she plots her sun sight. Verne usually took a ten o'clock sun sight and the noon sight. Rick took a series of star sights in the morning, as soon as the horizon was visible.

a native come into town from the bush with his bare ass showing. Everyday four women come down to the beach near where we are anchored and strip and take a bath.

August 7—We sailed from Luganville at noon and headed for Port Moresby under a light breeze.

August 8—We made good time all night. Ray caught a mahi mahi and made poisson cru. I took sun sights and worked out our position. I seem to be getting the knack of it. Toward evening we caught a tuna. Under mainsail and genoa, making six knots.

August 13—We've been at sea now for six days and are nine hundred miles closer to Port Moresby. The weather has been good. We have never had such good luck catching fish before. We got to the point where we threw the last one back. Now we have taken in the fishing line altogether. We were eating fried fish, baked fish, creamed fish, fish in milk, fish in butter, and fish in tomato sauce—morning, noon, and night. It was like those onions I bought in Nouméa. I ordered ten pounds of onions and seventy pounds of potatoes. The order got mixed up and we sailed with ten pounds of potatoes and seventy pounds of onions. Now we eat stewed onions, fried onions, baked onions, creamed onions, and even raw onions. Just a plain can of stew would taste good for a change. After this length of time at sea (which isn't really very long) everyone starts talking about what they would like most to eat. I want a big steak and green salad. Mel has lost a lot of weight this trip. She looks good.

August 15—Last night while changing tacks in a strong southeast wind, something went wrong and the mainsail ripped from leech to luff. The throat of the gaff broke loose from the mast and the gaff became fouled in the rigging and swung wildly from side to side. Verne had to climb up the ratlines to free it. What a night it was. We put up the storm trysail and staysail and continued on. Then we found water in the diesel and didn't dare use the engine, so we sailed into Port Moresby under storm trysail and genoa and dropped the anchor at 16:00. We made the passage from Luganville in eight days: the log read 1261 miles. Everybody's clothes were filthy, and there were no clean towels on board. We all needed a shower. And what did we find here? A wonderful yacht club with all the facilities. From what people said about Port Moresby, I didn't expect to like it, but we had one of our best times here. It's a small, clean city. The natives are the most colorful we have met. Most of the women are tattooed all over their bodies and faces, and those that come down from the bush are bare chested. The men have big holes cut in their ears so most of their ears look like they have been in a dog fight. The men wear earrings, necklaces, bracelets, and flowers in their hair. The men of the Mickeo tribe are quite handsome with their red lava lavas and big head of hair and fine features. The natives of the tribe that live in Port Moresby and do the housework for the Europeans are quite small—almost like pigmies.

    The wind howled the whole three weeks we were in Port Moresby, sometimes gusting up to 30 knots. On two different mornings we found that our 250 pound anchor had dragged and we were out in the middle of the bay. One night the schooner anchored next to us dragged her anchor and raked our taffrail with her bowsprit.

One day we moved over to the freighter wharf to take on water and stores. The wharf was packed with natives staring at us the whole two days we were there. We were never so glad to get out at anchor again. We bought a new anchor chain and picked up our mainsail—the repair was done well and cost only four pounds. Mel and I met three girls, Liz, Kae, and Di, at the yacht club and invited them over to meet the boys. We never lacked for friends while here. We were in the local paper and on the radio.

September 4—But we had to leave, so after picking up our clearance papers, we raised the anchor at 16:00 and headed for the Torres Strait. We wanted to sail out of the harbor but the wind was blowing right through the pass. Even with the engine on we barely made any headway, and then the engine heated up and began spewing black smoke and unburnt diesel out the exhaust. We were heading back to port when the temperature dropped, so we decided to try and get through the pass and raise the sails. We were successful and sailed all night in light winds and part of the next day until the wind dropped. Turning on the engine, we powered all that day and night.

September 6—We expected to see Bramble Cay Light this morning but the weather was misting and visibility was poor, so we missed it. We continued on dead reckoning and made our turn into the Great Northern Passage of the Torres Strait. The engine started heating up again but then the wind came up so we could set sail. We expected to see a low island but didn't sight a thing all day. Whenever the sun peeped out from behind a cloud, Verne or Rick took a sight. Each sight put us further to the east than our dead reckoning course, which indicated a strong current

The Outrigger

The outrigger canoe, with its tiki head on the bow, was finished in Nouméa, but the outrigger itself wasn't attached until Port Moresby. The photo shows the outrigger's maiden voyage with Fairweather's *deck crew, from the bow, Verne, Rick, Jon, and Ray.*

was running in the strait. Just before dusk, Ray sighted a spit of sand called Pearce Cay, so we finally knew where we were. The engine was still overheating, so we anchored in nine fathoms of water for the night. We got busy on the engine and got it working properly. It was a good feeling going to bed that night knowing where we were in the Torres Strait and knowing the engine was working. We kept an anchor watch all night but there was little wind and we didn't drag. We could see the light on Dalrymphle Ilet during the night. We opened a bottle of wine to celebrate my birthday the next day.

September 7—We anchored off Sue Ilet. Everyone wanted to go ashore but it was getting late so we all just jumped in sea for a swim and then went to bed.

September 8—We were up at daybreak and underway at 06:00. With the tide and current with us, we raced through the channel between Prince of Wales Island and Thursday Island and dropped the anchor off Thursday Island at 15:00. The log read 363 miles. The doctor was playing bowls so we had to wait until he finished before he came and cleared us. While waiting the boys went for a swim, which shocked the whole island. *Nobody* swims here because of the sharks, which are quite vicious. They are being killed every day off the pier. The doctor finally came and he found that our smallpox vaccinations had expired, so we made arrangements to renew them the next day.

The first thing I wanted to do on shore was get a big steak. In the sailing directions it says you can get all the fresh meat you want on Thursday Island. But what do we end up with? Fish and chips. Sue and Pat went to the movies while we went to the hotel bar. Women aren't allowed in the bar: they have to sit in the ladies' lounge if they want a beer. Mel and I really had them going because we refused to sit in the ladies' lounge and insisted on being in the pub. We won our point.

The wind howled through the anchorage the whole time we were here. The town itself reminded me of one of our old western cow towns, except for the cowboys and horses. There is not a horse on the island and some of the kids have never seen one. The people were all interested in our cruise. They couldn't get over a woman skipper sailing around the world with her four children. They think American women are something. And what a place to be during America's Cup race. These Australians have no doubt that they are going to win and we are sure taking a rubbing. If we win our name is mud, but if we lose we won't be able to live with them. The Australians are wonderful people, so much different from the New Zealanders. They are more like Americans but I think even friendlier. I'm glad we will be making a stop in Darwin.

September 12—We took on water at the wharf and then got underway at 07:15, heading for Darwin. It was a wild four days we spent on Thursday Island and I loved every minute of it. I would have stayed another week if the wind had stopped howling, but it was miserable at anchor and we got soaked every time we took the dinghy ashore.

The wind is light today and we are ghosting along at four knots. Not fast but very comfortable. I thought with that wind at Thursday Island we would be screaming along to Darwin, but the wind must just funnel through the anchorage because it is calm out here in the Arafura Sea. The supply ship came in Tuesday, so we were able to get fresh meat before we left. One thing they did have was cold beer.

September 19—We tied up at the wharf in Darwin at 18:00. The log read 702 miles. There were light winds all the way from Thursday Island. Monday night the wind died altogether and we powered the rest of the way to Darwin. What a lot of publicity we are getting! Tonight on Radio Australia from Sydney they are broadcasting a tape they made on board today. Last night we were on the local radio station, and today I was interviewed by two newspapers. It seems that an American yacht with a woman skipper is quite a news item.

We moved over to another wharf. While we were turning the boat around by hand, the current caught her, and as the tide came flooding in, we nearly got her stern caught under the wharf. Everyone was working, sweating in the heat, trying to fend her off. A photographer from a newspaper was snapping pictures like mad. He was having fun, but we sure weren't.

Two Australian destroyers tied up across from us, and Captain Parker of the *HMAS Quiberon* sent a messenger over with a special invitation to a party on board, so Mel and I didn't have to crash this one. They are headed for Singapore as well and offered to tow us there, so we asked them if they anchored at night. They were all a bunch of swell fellows.

Well, we found Darwin a very hot place with nice cold beer, but if we don't get out of here next week, we will have to stay for six months because of the weather. We took on fifteen cases of beer under bond for only 1.6 pounds a case. We couldn't get cigarettes unless we took 10,000.

From the Bowsprit

Sue and Pat liked to swing in the bo'sun's chair from the end of the main boom. They plunged into the sea every time Fairweather *rolled to leeward. In the photo, Jon is swinging in the bo'sun's chair from the bowsprit, getting soaked every time the bow dipped into a wave. Daily life aboard was simple but healthy, for the crew was rarely ill at sea, except Ray, who suffered from seasickness the first few days after leaving port.*

October 3—With good teamwork, we got underway very smartly at 07:00. Coming out of the harbor, we passed two Australian naval ships on the way in. We dipped our flag to them and they returned the courtesy. We powered out in the Timor Sea for twenty miles, turned off the engine, and raised the sails. We aren't going fast but a least we aren't going backwards.

Ray prepared a good tucker (as he calls it) today: ham, coleslaw, minted peas, and apple sauce. It brought to mind our last night in port when the boys visited a freighter. The crew of the freighter asked what we ate and the boys said our stores consisted of beer and vitamin pills. They felt so sorry for the boys that they stuffed them with all kinds of food.

October 6—I came on watch this morning, and when the sun came up, I sighted Timor. Every night we are on the starboard tack and every day on the port tack. We have worked our way up north to Timor. Now we are working our way to the southwest.

October 9—Sighted Timor again this morning. We have logged 500 miles but have made good only 350. We are taking the route through the Indian Ocean. It has been a very relaxing time this past week. Pat spends his free time building boats. Sue spends hers baking cookies. It's only noon—four hours before cocktail hour.

October 10—We have gone 520 miles in eight days. Verne and Ray rigged the bo'sun's chair from the main boom out over the water and the kids had fun swinging from it and swimming—then the wind came up and we got under way at six knots. Ray made a kite and we all told him it wouldn't fly but it did and was flying beautifully until it took a nose dive and sank. Pat then spent the afternoon making one but the wind was too strong for him to fly it. Mel is on watch and just gave a loud scream. Rushing up on deck she said a huge fish just spit at her and got her all wet.

October 14—We are lying off Bali, waiting for daylight before heading into the harbor at Benoa. The wind has been fair the past four days, and we averaged 150 miles a day. Tonight there is no wind and a rolling sea. There are two million people on Bali but all we can see is a single light. During the night we drifted into what seemed to be breakers on a reef. The water was boiling all around us, and it was spooky as hell. We powered out of it, and realized only later that it was caused by the tide and current flowing between Bali and Lombok.

October 15—What a sight greeted us this morning as we got underway. There were over two hundred double-outrigger boats with lateen sails. The hulls were beautifully carved and painted. We thought they were a racing fleet until we saw them all fishing. As we came to the entrance of the channel into Benoa, we couldn't figure out the buoy system. In the *Sailing Directions* it says the buoys are painted red and green, but in fact they were all rusted and some of them looked like bird cages. So we laid off and waited for a pilot boat that never came. About an hour later, a freighter that was in the harbor came out through the channel. So we marked her course and then started through ourselves. We were doing fine until the last bird cage, which we started passing on the wrong side. An English tanker in the harbor started blowing her whistle and Verne in the cross trees saw the reef. Rick made a sharp turn to starboard and we nearly took the bird cage with us as we just missed the reef. We dropped the anchor at 15:00. The log read 1,076 miles. About half an hour after dropping anchor, a launch came out with the doctor, port authorities, immigration, navy, plus their assistants. All our papers were in order and they were all very polite and courteous. We offered them a beer which they took but, by the way they handled the bottle, I don't think they drank beer.

Then we moved over to another anchorage and the English tanker started giving us flag signals. So after getting the dinghy over the side, Ray, Verne, Mel, and I went over to see what they were signaling. They invited us aboard for a beer. Mel and I took showers and washed our hair. They were leaving at five or we would probably still be there.

Next day we went into Denpasar, which is five miles away. First we had to clear through the navy base at Benoa and fill out a form for exchanging money. The official in charge said the rate of exchange was 300 rupiahs to the Australian pound. He said that was double the regular rate of exchange because we are tourists. (Later, at the bank, we found that the official rate of exchange was 400 rupiahs to the pound.) We got a ride in a truck to town. It was a fascinating ride: both sides of the road are just one continuous village all the way into Denpasar. There are temples everywhere, and women, young and old, carry a fantastic amount of weight on their heads. Most of the older women are bare-chested. Men carry pigs in circular bamboo cages. Men also take the place of horses, pulling carts loaded with just about everything imaginable.

We wandered all over town, trying to see everything. While we were having lunch in a small café (where we couldn't read the menu), a man came up to Verne and handed him a note saying, "I'm a money changer. I will give you 800 rupiahs for one pound." Black market! Just what the official in Benoa said to avoid. But this man was offering double the official bank rate. So Verne set up a deal for the next day. Our meal with beer came to 25 cents apiece. We couldn't get a bus back to Benoa and didn't have enough money for a taxi, so we started walking back. I bought eggs for two cents apiece, tomatoes for one cent, and a loaf of bread for three cents.

Next day Jon stayed on the boat and we started for town again. Again we got a ride right away. We met Mada Budi and he took us on a bus to Kangklang, about 30 miles inland. We bought some wood carvings for half what they cost in Denpasar. Then we couldn't get a bus back, and our guide wanted us to take a taxi for 1,100 rupiahs. He came down to 900 but we still said no. Then we saw a truck loading up and asked the driver for a ride. He took us and 20 women and all their supplies. On the way back we had to pull over, get off the truck, and line up at the edge of the road, as Sukarno and the President of Mexico drove by. When we got back to the Bali Hotel, we began discussing how we were going to get back to Benoa. Then three men at the next table, who overheard us, offered us their car and driver. They were with the Sukarno crowd. They drove us out and offered to pick us up in the morning to see the parade given in honor of the President of Mexico. So in the morning we went into town again. The parade was really interesting but I was so tired I couldn't really enjoy the day. Ray and I took a pony cart back to Benoa for 50 cents.

October 23—I got clearance from immigration, the harbor master, and the navy, and we left Benoa at 09:00. Five minutes later we missed the channel and went aground. The bird cages that marked the channel were simply ambiguous. Tide was going out so we had to sit there until it came back in at night. At low tide we were lying over on our side, so Verne painted in the water line. The navy and a pilot came out and showed us a chart of the channel. We politely pointed out that two channel buoys were missing. That night, just before high tide, we started trying to get off the reef. We swung the main boom back and forth to rock the boat. At slack water we started to move back into the channel. It was pitch black and we couldn't see a thing, so we headed back toward the harbor, guided by the light of a freighter tied to the wharf. Two minutes later we were aground on the other side of the channel. We set a stern anchor and tried to pull off with it and the engine. No luck. So we sat the night out, waiting for the tide in the morning. This time the reef was uneven and we were worried we may crack a plank when the boat settles on her side, but the boat heeled very little during the night. The tide was higher in the morning and we backed off with very little trouble. Verne dove down to check the bottom, and when he came up he said the paint wasn't even scratched.

October 25—We sailed east of Bali and into the Java Sea, heading for Selat Madura. We had good winds yesterday and last night but they have failed this morning. After going aground in Benoa, Rick is continually checking our position. We heard on the radio last night about the Cuban

Missile Crisis. We are all anxious to learn the outcome, if the Americans will really sink a Russian ship carrying war supplies.

October 26—We stood off the mouth of East Gat Channel all day, waiting for a pilot to come out and bring us into Surabaya. All types of sailing boats and warships sailed around us.

October 27—We followed the buoys and anchored in the roadstead in Surabaya at 12:00. The log read 275 miles. We waited to be cleared, but no one took notice of us. The next day we saw customs running around clearing three big freighters, so we jiggled our quarantine flag to draw their attention. It worked. The doctor and customs came aboard. Later they sent us a pilot to take us to the yacht club. A squall hit us while we were making our way in. As we approached the yacht club, the pilot said to tie up in a berth that we could see already had a boat in it. Next he said to tie up to a police launch (which we thought was an even worse idea). Then a man came out in a small speed boat and said to drop anchor and tie stern-to at the floating dock. What a mess. And it was pouring rain the whole time. We were assured at the yacht club that there was fifteen feet of water at low tide. We draw eight feet and we sat on the bottom at each low tide—that was the shallowest fifteen feet I ever saw. But aside from that, everything was perfect and the people were very hospitable. The yacht club committee, Major Natakusuma, Mr. Munter, and Mr. call-me-Bless Bleszynski, met us and offered us the facilities of the club, which included not only a swimming pool and showers but also a laundry service. That night the club gave us an Indonesian dinner.

Bless (Mr. Bleszynski) set up a train trip to Borabudbud temple in Jogakarta for us. I didn't realize it was clear across Java on the Indian Ocean side of the island. He picked us up at 05:00 and found our seats on the train. There was a car waiting for us with a sign that read "Kaptan Adam" on the windshield. We spent the night up in the mountains at a lodge. It was cool and comfortable, in fact it was so cool we all caught colds. We got the third class train back to Surabaya. What a long miserable trip. No breakfast or lunch, and it was hot and crowded.

We met Winks and Bill Welkens working on the Westinghouse power plant project. Mel and I had a hot bath and dinner at their house. The next day, Bill Welkens sent his car and driver over for our use. I mentioned to him that I wanted to purchase some beer. The next morning, five cases of beer were delivered to the boat, plus eggs and bread. He wanted us to stay in the worst way but we were already cleared for Djakarta and I thought it was best to leave as planned, so we departed at 09:00. I can truthfully say that Surabaya has been our most pleasant port of call in terms of friendship and generosity of the people.

November 7—There's no wind, so we are under power. But since we paid only 50 cents a gallon for diesel in Surabaya, we can easily power all the way to Djakarta. There are many small boats (parus) out fishing. Coming up close to them in the morning, we could smell their breakfast cooking. One night we nearly ran one down. They carry no lights at night and we were almost upon this one before he could light a fire and wave us off.

November 9—We sailed into Djakarta harbor and anchored in front of the yacht club at 15:00. The log read 367 miles. It's no longer a private club. The army has taken it over and it's now for public use. Never saw a port official the whole time we were in Djakarta. Captain Sceato of the Indonesian Air Force took care of all our papers, even to getting our visas extended. Next morning the vice-commodore of the yacht club, Ismet, came down to the boat, and invited us for lunch at his house. He got a bus for Sunday and took us up into the mountains where it is cool. In contrast to the cool and green mountains, Djakarta is a hot and dirty city, just swarming with people. The city is on the sea with a large canal running through the main part of it. The water in the canal is filthy, but still, people line the banks washing their clothes, brushing their teeth, and even using it for a toilet. The food is good, but it's perhaps not surprising that we are all coming down with a case of diarrhea.

Bless (Mr. Bleszynski) showed up Monday with his Chinese girlfriend. What an attractive woman she is and what a character he is. He tried to convince me it would be better to get work done on the boat back in Surabaya instead of Singapore. The crew was a little worried that he had convinced me.

November 15—We raised the anchor at 15:00 and headed for Singapore. We powered north through Stalze Strait into the South China Sea. No wind. The only time we can sail is when a squall comes up. The squalls are averaging four per day now, but the wind drops down as soon as they pass.

November 20—A fair wind has come up, but it's still very hot. We will cross the equator at approximately midnight and should reach Singapore by tomorrow afternoon.

Baggywrinkle

Fairweather *carried baggywrinkle on her rigging to prevent the sails from chafing against the shrouds. The baggywrinkle was made from old manila rope, and making it was a simple task that the crew usually did at sea. In the photo, Verne is on the topmast, setting the topsail in light weather.*

Indian Ocean

November 21—When I came on watch at 05:30, I saw that we are in the Singapore Strait. We dropped the anchor in front of the Royal Singapore Yacht Club at 11:00. The log read 654 miles. We had no courtesy flag for Malaya but noticed the other ships carrying a flag similar to the Indonesian one with a half moon and five stars. In five minutes we had a Malayan flag but with only one star. It didn't seem to bother anyone. So we sat on the boat with only four bottles of beer left, waiting for immigration and customs. There were all kinds of official boats running around but they completely ignored us. At 13:00 Ray and I got in the dinghy and went over to the yacht club. Mr. Jack Hughes met us at the landing, showed us around, and bought us a beer. He said not to worry about customs. They don't care whether we are here or not. But I sent Ray back for the rest of the crew and then went to immigration and got cleared.

The city of Singapore is just what I expected: narrow streets with Chinese stores, merchants on the side walk selling their wares, and money changers everywhere, waiting for business. Everyone wants to bargain. You can't buy a handkerchief without haggling over it. I made arrangements to have the boat hauled out at Quam Bee Slipway. We moved over to the boatyard and we were glad to get

Repairs

Suttie contracted with Ming at the Quam Bee boatyard to have Fairweather's *taffrail replaced with a new one made of teak. It was a contract formalized with a handshake. When the workmen began pulling up the old taffrail, they found dry rot in the stern.* Fairweather *was at anchor (and without electricity). In any case, Ming's workmen used only hand tools, such as an adz, to form the wood. In the photo, the stern planks have been removed, exposing the lazarette. In the photo, Jon watches Rick untie the dinghy's painter. To the left and right are two woodworkers.*

away from the anchorage in front of the yacht club because they were racing their small boats every day and we always seemed to be in the way. We tied up next to the *Sea Nymph*, a 63-foot powerboat with a tall mast added as an afterthought. The *Sea Nymph* is owned by John Calvert, a stage magician and former owner of the schooner *Sea Fox*. He tells fantastic stories about everything. He has two girls on board who are in his show. He wants Jon and Mel for his show when he sails up to Penang. It should be interesting for them.

December 17—After having the bottom scraped and painted, we moved over to the anchorage in front of the Singapore Boatel. At the boatyard, Quam Bee told some interesting stories about the Indonesian pirates. He said that they would come alongside of his fishing boat and steal everything that wasn't nailed down. He stopped that by dropping homemade bombs—made from dynamite—in a boat that came along side, sinking it.

December 25—Sue got a watch and Pat a bike, so I guess they enjoyed their day. The carpenters came today and started pulling up the taffrail and found a lot of dry rot in the stern. Mr. Noon (Tom), the boss, asked for some hot water so I gave him the tea kettle. Then I saw that they had no tea and were drinking just hot water for lunch. Engine repaired.

May 13, 1963—Released the lines at 06:00 and left Singapore for Penang. We spend six months in Singapore and enjoyed every bit of it. Ming and his crew of woodworkers did a beautiful job on the boat: they replaced the rotten stern planks, built a new teak taffrail, and carved new locker doors, all with hand tools. Rick designed a square sail for crossing the Indian Ocean, and we tried it out, sending Jon and Verne aloft. It worked well, at least in the calm water of Singapore Strait. The Singapore Swimming Club was a life saver for Sue and Pat and they spent most of their time there.

We have two friends on board for as far as Penang—Ethel Boyals and Bob Miller. The passage up the Malacca Strait has been quiet and relaxing. An Indonesian gunboat bore down on us and gave us the once over. It looked like they had Russian technicians on board for a crew. We had to hove-to at night during the squalls.

May 17—We powered through the channel into Penang harbor and dropped anchor at 15:00 next to the *Via Vita*, a former minesweeper, now used as a yacht. The log read 354 miles. The *Via Vita* has showers that they invited us to use. Bob Miller took us out for a fabulous Chinese dinner—if you like Chinese food. They served a beautiful suckling pig and all we were supposed to eat was the skin. It was impossible to cut the meat with chopsticks. I got in touch with Felix Hill, manager of Chartered Bank, and spent Sunday touring Penang. It's a beautiful island but our anchorage in Penang harbor is miserable: we spent half of our time fending off freighters because of the tide and strong current that runs between Penang and the mainland.

May 25—We are ready to leave Penang for the Nicobar Islands. I had to run back and forth to get our clearance, but there was no trouble with customs about the beer and cigarettes. We raised the anchor at 16:30, powered out of the harbor, and raised the sails.

Indian Ocean

May 26—Penang is still in sight astern. Turned on the engine. The wind came up in the evening, but it wasn't steady or reliable.

May 27—Still no wind, very hot, still under power.

May 28—Light winds from the southwest. While on watch at 19:00, the wind came up. We put the boat on the starboard tack, then bam! The wind jumped to 40 knots. We had to run with it—back to Penang—until we could shorten sail. The genoa sheet broke, and we hove-to for the night.

May 29—Winds are still strong this morning. We got sails up on port tack, and we are beating to windward but not making much headway. The genoa sheet broke again. We set the staysail. We have been in port too long. I'd forgotten how miserable and nasty the sea can be. Welcome to the Indian Ocean.

May 30—Sailing under staysail and storm trysail. It's blowing hard from the southwest. At noon we raised the foresail and started making about four knots. We need to tack south soon in order to make Great Nicobar Island.

May 31—Wind still blowing hard. We are making very little headway: for every five miles we gain, we get blown back four. Hove-to again. The yardarm on the foremast is too heavy for this head wind. The boys unrigged it and with difficulty lowered it to the deck.

June 1—We had a knock-down on Jon's watch. The starboard deck was under water, up to the cabin top. As we released the sheets and ran down wind, we were going so fast that the drive shaft came uncoupled. Boys fixed it temporarily. Now under storm sails again. We are thirty miles from Nicobar Island but can't see it. We haven't seen

Great Nicobar

The edge of a typhoon hit Fairweather *in the Andaman Sea, on the passage from Penang to Nicobar. The crew decided to lighten the schooner as much as possible, so they unrigged the square sail and abandon the outrigger canoe on the beach in Nicobar. In the photo, two Nicobar Islanders have taken possession of the outrigger, which they later used to paddled out to* Fairweather *anchored in the bay.*

the sun in five days. Wind died down in the night, so we turned on the engine, hoping to make some headway.

June 5—The sun came out, so we were able to fix our position. It seems that we have been going backwards. We have logged 700 miles since leaving Penang and yet we are in the same position we were in eight days ago. The northeast current is pushing us faster than we are sailing. In the night the jib throat tore out, and then the staysail clew ripped out. We had to hove-to for the night. The next night the jib sheet parted and the sail ripped. The shackle on the staysail sheet broke. We gained eight miles and lost ten.

June 7—We are off Great Nicobar Island. No wind. We turned on the engine. One cylinder is broken and makes a horrible noise but the engine kept going at a slow speed. We anchored in Trinkat Champhong Bay at 16:30. The log read 907 miles (Nicobar is 360 miles from Penang). The island is a beautiful emerald-green and there is no sign of civilization. We went ashore and just ran up and down the white sandy beach. We all slept soundly that night.

June 8—Jon, Verne, Sue, and Pat went hiking today. Ray, Rick, Mel, and I went skin diving this afternoon on the other side of the bay. The water is crystal clear. Ray speared all types and colors of fish. Rick got a little one. We took them to the beach with some potatoes, carrots and beer, threw the potatoes in the fire, then wrapped the fish and carrots in tinfoil and baked them. We were a little cautious about the fish being poisonous. We didn't eat the red polka-dotted or yellow and black stripped ones. No one got sick. Best fish dinner we ever had. Boy, it's good to be back on land for a while.

June 10—We went spear fishing again and got eight nice sized fish and one large lobster. We saw two natives on the beach.

June 11—Jon, Ray, and Verne brought back 15 lobsters for breakfast. What a feast. We cleaned the boat up and put the out-rigger canoe the boys built over the side. It had become nothing more than a place to store junk. The boys left the canoe on the beach for the natives. When we saw a fire and went over to investigate, we met the two natives. They had on only a loincloth and looked like true primitives. We tried to explain to them that the canoe was for them.

June 12—While sanding and varnishing in the morning, we noticed that the natives were working on the canoe. In the afternoon we went ashore to investigate. They had made a very good outrigger for the canoe, and they seemed friendlier than before, although they didn't talk at all. They may have thought trying to talk to us was pointless. Later they launched the canoe and paddled along the beach, and then they came out to *Fairweather*. There were two of them, a man and a boy, and they just sat in the canoe, holding on to the side of *Fairweather*. First we gave them some pineapple juice. One of them said something and it sounded like "sugar," so we gave them some. Rick gave them some fish hooks, and Mel gave one of them her red hat, and Verne gave them a bayonet. Then the man stood up and pointed to the rag he was wearing, so Ray gave them an orange pareo. This all happened in silence, like a ceremony. After that they left. They chewed betel nut and their mouths were all red and their teeth rotten. They

Indian Ocean

didn't look like any of the people in Singapore or Penang: not Chinese, Indian, or Malayan (or white for that matter).

June 13—Boys went spear fishing this morning. Pat speared a lobster. Was he excited. We left the anchorage at 11:00 for the bay at Laful, about five miles up the coast. There was a river there and we wanted to pick up some fresh water. A squall blew in as we left and hid the land, so we ended up going right past the bay. We finally found the bay and dropped the anchor at 16:00. We went ashore to look at the river, and when we got there, we jumped in, clothes and all. Then we took the dinghy up the river, looking for cleaner water. What an eerie place, like a movie set. We expected to see crocodiles (the river is called Crocodile River), but we didn't see a thing. The river had a rotten smell to it, so we didn't take on any water.

June 15—We raised the anchor and sailed out of Laful at 08:00, heading north for the St. George Passage between Great Nicobar and Little Nicobar Islands. There was a moderate head wind, and as we were tacking through the passage, we noticed an outrigger canoe with eight natives that came out from Great Nicobar. They were paddling vigorously, trying to intercept us. After a short discussion, we decided that they didn't have anything we wanted, and so we tacked to avoid them. We had to tack between the islands a few more times, and each time the outrigger was closer, eventually coming within a hundred yards of us. Then we tacked one last time, sailed into the Indian Ocean and left them behind.

June 22—Noon position:

Cruising

Fairweather *had a ship's clock that chimed the quarter hour. In the photo, it is late afternoon, probably about 16:00 or eight bells. Ray and Mel are lying on deck and Verne is lying on the main cabin top (Rick is at the helm). The wind is too far forward of the beam to carry the flying fisherman, so it and its sheets are on deck, ready to be reset as soon as the wind shifts. This is cruising under sail.*

Indian Ocean

Lat. 1° 30" N
Long. 92° 26" E

It has been a week of very relaxing sailing. On Verne's watch we caught a fish that looked like a skinny tuna, about 20 pounds. Verne opened up its stomach and found two long tape worms inside. No wonder it was skinny.
June 27—Noon position:

Lat. 3° 58" S
Long. 90° 50" E

We are still heading south, looking for the southeast trades. No wind for the last two days, but there have been numerous squalls that keep us moving right along. This morning we caught a big tuna, about forty pounds.
July 1—The wind came around to the south-southeast. We are now in the trades and heading west.
July 7—We are 300 miles from Diego Garcia in the Chagos Archipelago. We have a lottery for when we sight land.
July 9—We sighted Diego Garcia at 17:30. It was on my watch so I won the lottery. The wind picked up yesterday and we made good time. We hove-to for the night, and now everyone is getting cleaned up to go ashore in the morning.
The wind came up strong during the night and it's blowing right out the pass, so it's impossible to make it into the anchorage. We hove-to on the other tack, hoping for better weather in the morning. The waves are monstrous, and we are slowly drifting toward the Great Chagos Bank.

July 11—It's still blowing hard, and we couldn't see the island in the morning, so we had to decide to either sit it out one more day, or head for the Seychelles. There was little room to maneuver and the Great Chagos Bank is no place to be lost in. So we set sail and headed west. Rick was continually taking sun sights, which was very difficult because the horizon was often hidden behind the monstrous waves. It was a very nervous day. Then we sighted Egbert Island in the afternoon and were able to fix our position. Now we have another thousand miles to go.

July 16—We crossed longitude 57° 40" E. We are half way around the world from San Francisco.

July 18—We sighted Frigate Island in the Seychelles yesterday at 10:00 and hove-to for the night. We had good trade winds for the past week and caught a fish nearly every day, so it was a pleasant passage. The pilot boat came out and led us through the pass at Mahé and into the inner harbor where we tied up stern-to. The log read 3117 miles. We were thirty-three days at sea, by far our longest passage. And what a relief it is to be on an even keel again. The Captain Young's ketch, *Diana*, is tied next to us. And what else do we find here a thousand miles from nowhere? A hundred Americans sent from the Bay Area to set up a tracking station—by RCA and Philco of Palo Alto. It's like being at home on a tropical island. And Mahé is very tropical and beautiful. The natives are overly friendly. It's something like Tahiti—parties going on all the time. But the weather has been miserable with only two nice days in two weeks. The first nice day I rode around the island on a motorcycle with Ray Manning. The second nice day we had a beach party at sunset. I had to wire to Mombasa for

Indian Ocean

a fuel injector for the engine, and we will have to stay here until it arrives on the ship that comes through here every two weeks.

August 9—The fuel injector arrived in the mail today. A local customs official, in a very white uniform, brought the package out to the boat and wanted to know who "authorized" importing it into the Seychelles. Rick pointed to the stamps on the package and said, "the Queen of England." That made the official smile and he handed the package to Rick.

August 15—We left Mahé for Zanzibar at noon. A local trading schooner had her anchor on top of ours and we had a devil of a time breaking ours loose. We burnt out three fuses on the anchor winch trying to raise both of them. We were delayed two hours getting out of the harbor. But without question Mahé has been one of our best ports of call. Sue and Pat wanted to stay here forever. I also had a strong inclination to stay.

August 21—After six days of fair winds, we sailed into Zanzibar and dropped anchor in front of the sailing club. The log read 977 miles. Since we arrived between 14:00 and 16:00, we were charged an extra five shillings for health and immigration. The friendliness of the Europeans was the best we have encountered. Something was going on every day for the whole crew. People came out to the boat every day. The town of Zanzibar is very exotic, with narrow alleyways and Indian shopkeepers. It was another port no one wanted to leave.

August 29—We put on a show, sailing off the anchor at 09:00. The whole sailing club was going to escort us out, but they didn't believe me when I said we were leaving at

Savo Royal National Park

The entire crew went on Rick and Mel's honeymoon to the Savo Royal National Park (Kenya was still British in 1963). In the photo, Rick is feeding a monkey, but what the photo doesn't show is that the rest of the monkey troop is raiding the crew's lunch basket.

Indian Ocean

09:00. In Zanzibar 09:00 means 10:00 or 11:00. Three boats managed to catch us as we were leaving and were sailing circles around us until we made the turn into the English Pass and raised all our sails. At that point we left them all astern. We are heading for Mombasa, 150 miles to the north.

August 30—There was very little wind, but although we were making only two knots under sail, the current was pushing us along at three more knots, so we arrived in Mombasa at noon. The log read 103 miles. In order to speed up our clearance, the harbor master in Zanzibar called the harbor master in Mombasa to say we were arriving at noon on Friday. We have been here one week now and no one has bothered to clear us. We finally took down the quarantine flag yesterday. Jon and I went up into the bush in a Land Rover with Lynn to look at sable and elephants. We saw three herds of sable but no elephants. Then we watched Lynn catch butterflies. He has net traps set along the road, and he puts a mixture of rotten bananas and rum in the bottom of the traps. The butterflies are attracted to the mixture and end up getting drunk. That's when Lynn picks them up. We also caught a bunch of ticks.

September 16— Rick came to me this morning and told me he and Mel were getting married this afternoon. Well, what could I say, except that I would like to be there. Mel didn't want me to know for fear I would send her home. I felt she has been a part of the family for so long now that it didn't make any difference. The question was where we should be seven months from now, when she has the baby.

September 19—Of course we all went on Rick and Mel's honeymoon. I hired a Peugeot limousine, and we stored our gear on top and took off for the Savo Royal National Park at 06:00. We booked at the Kitani Lodge for 20 shillings and brought our own food. When we went in through the Voi Gate, we were met by a baby hippo and elephant. And while driving through the park the rest of the day we saw numerous other animals: monkeys, baboons, caracals, jackals, zebras, rhinoceros, wart hogs, hippopotamuses, giraffes, buffaloes, seven different types of antelopes, elephants, dik-diks, and ostriches. The number of animals was impressive. The climax of the day was seeing a rhino ahead on the road. We stopped while he crossed the road, and then we proceeded on. Just as we passed him, he took out after us. We speeded up to 30 miles an hour (on the dirt road) and he was next to us on the right, hooking his heavy head toward the car. The road made a turn to the left and he kept going straight. I don't know what would have happened if the road had turned to the right. We went to the Kilaguni Lodge for a drink after that and later headed for the Kitani Lodge. They had excellent accommodations at the lodge, and sitting on our veranda, we could see Kilimanjaro in the distance. That evening we sat in the dark and watched the animals go down to the water hole.

The next morning we went out at dawn and there were animals everywhere. We stopped near a bull elephant, and Verne and Ray got out of the car to take a picture. After taking a picture, Verne roared, trying to imitate an elephant. The bull elephant looked up, raised his trunk and started flapping his ears, and then he bellowed and charged. We left in a hurry, with Verne jumping in while the car was already moving. We put 500 miles on the car and everyone enjoyed the honeymoon.

Indian Ocean

September 24—We had the engine stripped down and taken out of the boat to be overhauled. Now it's back in and running smoothly for the first time in months (cost $900). I made arrangements to come up to the wharf to pick up diesel and water. The night before, the yacht club gave us a going away party and presented us with its club burgee. Rick stood up on a stool and gave a speech saying how much we enjoyed their hospitality and friendship. So at 14:00 we slipped the lines and headed out of Mombasa for Aden. As we passed the yacht club, they had signal flags flying, wishing us bon voyage. It made us feel good to think they thought well of us. Outside the channel, Dicksie was in his sail boat waiting to take pictures of us under full sail. Then he came along side and gave me the roll of film. The sea is calm and the wind light from east-southeast.

September 25—We're getting close to the equator again. There is a lot of rain and squalls. Ray put a wrench on the drive shaft to stop it from rotating, and now it's so quiet below deck it feels like we are hove-to. I have to run up on deck every so often to see if we are moving. It's a very strange feeling not hearing the prop spin. The sound was how I could estimate our speed.

September 26—The sun came out and Verne got a noon sight. The sun is right over the equator now and at noon bringing the sun down to the horizon is difficult. The sight was not very accurate.

September 27—Winds are light but we are averaging 150 knots a day because of the strong current along the African coast. Wind is behind us and causes *Fairweather* to roll from rail-to-rail. With my bunk athwart ships, it is very uncomfortable trying to sleep.

October 2—We rounded Ras Guardafui at 05:00 and now we are in the Gulf of Aden. No wind last night or the night before, so we are under power. Then the wind came up at 06:00 and we are under sail. So far it's been very pleasant sailing up the African coast: light winds, calm seas, and a current going our way. There were a few squalls in the vicinity of the equator, but otherwise the weather has been good.

October 5—We arrived in Aden and anchored off the Aden Yacht Club at 16:00. The log read 1289 miles, but because of the current, the distance actually traveled was 1497 miles. Well, Aden is like they said—*hot.* The water in the pipe along the pier is so hot that we have to wait until three in the morning to take a shower. The Aden Yacht Club is in the middle of nowhere. We were putting the dinghy over the side, when three racing boats came by and we invited the crews aboard. They were R.A.F. members and they had a yacht club around the island. They suggested we bring *Fairweather* over there where it was much more convenient for getting into town, so the next morning at high tide we moved over. We took the bus into town and found it flooded with duty-free merchandise. Everything is cheap if you are in the market for cameras, watches, radios, and so forth, but when it comes to food or supplies for the boat, the prices are exorbitant.

Since this is a Muslim country, their day of worship is Friday, while Sunday is just an ordinary working day. The Arab women conceal their faces behind a thin, colored scarf that allows them to see. And they wear a long black robe that covers them from head to toe, a type of burka. You can see their toes, and it seems that the Arab men use the toes to recognize the women—though it's not really clear how they are able to do that. We were planning to stay in Aden until the first of November, when the tides are low so we could tie the boat up to the dock and paint the bottom, but after one week, we are ready to leave.

October 19—We left Aden at 09:00. It was a disappointing port of call. I don't know whether it was the heat or just the surrounding atmosphere, but we found the place unpleasant. So now we have the Red Sea before us. We had good wind until 05:00 when it dropped completely and we turned on the engine. Wind came up again after five hours and we are under sail again. Of all things to go wrong on this passage, it had to be our most important instrument: the compass. It developed a leak. We filled it with alcohol, but a bubble continued to form at the top and the compass card kept getting stuck, making it difficult to steer a course. Then the stove sprung a leak and spouted flames all over the galley. Rick got the fire extinguisher and put it out.

October 21—We are averaging 100 miles a day with light winds from the south-southeast. Freighters pass us day and night, going both directions, so we must be in the shipping lanes. Now the compass fogs up in the evening at about 18:00, making it almost impossible to see the course. Ships have been flashing signals at us at night, usually saying that our lights are not working properly. They must take us for a much larger ship because of the height of our top-mast light.

October 25—We entered Port Sudan under sail at 14:00. The pilot came out to meet us and brought us up to a buoy. All ships over 10 tons must have a pilot at a cost of four pounds (twelve dollars). Any movement in the harbor requires a pilot at a cost of four pounds. Tying to the buoy cost one pound per day. Having the pilot boat catch the line to tie us to the buoy cost five pounds. They waived that for me thank goodness. Then there were harbor charges, light dues, and then the pilot again for leaving the harbor. So after four days in Port Sudan it cost us forty dollars.

The harbor master, Jim Cole, introduced us to the English Club (Red Sea Club) which made our stay bearable. We never saw a native woman in town. They stay out of the town in their homes with high walls around them. The men dress in long, white gowns.

October 28—We took on four barrels of extra diesel on deck in anticipation of powering up to Port Suez. The pilot came aboard at 16:00. At the wharf there was a barge in front of us and a tug boat behind, and the wind was holding us to the wharf. The pilot had two pilot boats pull us away from the wharf, but instead of pulling us straight out, they pulled us astern into the tug, damaging the fisherman vang. I made them understand that they should let us go, so we would get out under our own power.

The wind was strong from northeast and the seas were high. We were under power but not making any headway into the wind. So we fell off, raised the sails, and started tacking across to the Arabian coast. While crossing the shipping lanes, we had to dodge four freighters, which meant we had to hove-to while they passed. The genoa sheet broke. The next night we headed back to the African coast on the starboard tack. The jib sheet broke.

Indian Ocean

October 31—The wind died down and the seas were calm enough to power, so we were able to make some headway on a direct course.

November 2—The wind came up last night from north-northwest, blowing strong. We were on the port tack, heading toward the Arabian coast. At noon we were within ten miles of the reefs. We tacked to starboard and headed back toward the African coast. The genoa sheet broke three times last night. It's better that the genoa sheet breaks than the sail rips or that something else happens.

November 3—The star sights this morning showed that we are making better progress than expected. We made forty miles up the Red Sea out of the last one-hundred sailed. We are close to the 24th latitude, and it's getting cooler all the time.

November 4—We are making very little progress. Sighted the same island off the African coast this morning that we saw yesterday. Miles made good—24. On the port tack heading toward the Arabian coast again. In the shipping lane the freighters are all lined up and closer together now. We had to turn on the bright spreader lights last night to keep from being run down. A freighter started flashing signals at us, which we couldn't read. Today Ray rigged up a device with two flashlight batteries and a small bulb, and he and Pat are practicing Morse code.

November 10—Wind and seas finally dropped enough for us to power on a direct course again, and we made good time as we approached the Gulf of Suez. But as we came to Jabal Channel at the southern entrance of the Gulf early Friday morning, the wind was blowing hard and the seas were high. Hove-to all morning, hoping the seas would calm down, but they only got worse. So we powered behind Shadwan Island to anchor and wait for calmer weather. Shadwan Island is barren—not a blade of grass on it. We hiked around on it the first day. Ray, Pat, and Rick went spear fishing. Ray got some big parrot fish. Pat speared an armored-type fish with square sides and Rick speared a stingray that flopped around in the dinghy and stung him on the hand.

We've had a good rest, but we are running out of food and are anxious to get moving. The wind has dropped slightly and we will try to get out today. It is very hazy and has been since we have been here. We raised the anchor at 12:30 and made for the Shadwan Channel, which gave us a little protection from the wind before entering the Gulf of Suez. But it was blowing as strong as ever in the gulf. We spent the whole night and morning trying to pass the light on Ashrafi Island.

November 11—We were not making any progress, so we powered over to Umm el Kiman and anchored behind a sand spit. From there we could see the gulf, so we decided to wait until the wind died down, or our food gave out.

November 12—We investigated the old ruins on the shore. Ray, Pat, and I went hiking, looking for signs of goats. Rick, Ray, and Sue went spear fishing—Sue spearing her first fish. While cleaning the fish on deck, a large ten foot manta ray swam by with three sharks. That ended our spear fishing.

November 13—The wind died down and so we got underway at 06:00. Waves were small and we made good time in the morning. Then the wind and seas came up again. We are averaging 30 miles a day.

Indian Ocean

November 15—We anchored at Abu Zenima on the eastern coast at 15:00. We were hove-to all morning off the African coast and the wind blew us over here. Mel, Jon, and Ray went ashore to try and buy some food. I haven't paid enough attention to our provisions because I haven't been doing any of the cooking since New Zealand, and now we are running out of basic items, so I need to keep a better eye on that. Mel hasn't been able to understand cruising, and she will be very busy when we get to Cyprus, so I'll take over cooking again.

Mel, Jon, and Ray came back with potatoes, eggs, butter, candy, and cookies. What a feast.

November 16—We raised the anchor at 09:00 and headed across the gulf again. It was calm when we were anchored, but the wind in the gulf was strong. When the wind shifted to the north, we made for Mansa el Lemet and dropped the anchor at 15:00. From the chart it looked like a perfectly protected cove, but it proved to be otherwise—white caps and howling wind. We are fifty-five miles from Port Suez.

November 17—Ray, Pat, and I went ashore and hiked over to some buildings, hoping to buy some bread. No luck. No one spoke English and the building that was under construction was a hotel. While we were hiking back to the dinghy, an Egyptian in uniform, riding a camel and carrying a gun, hailed us. He wanted our passes (we think). From what we could make out, he had called Suez about us and wanted to check our passes. We said they were on the boat, so he rode back to the dinghy with us. He wanted one of us to stay on shore with him while the rest returned to the boat, but we all got in the dinghy and shoved off.

The guy was angry and we were afraid he would draw his gun but he didn't. When we got back to the boat we sat and watch him through the glasses. He was sitting on the beach waiting for us. When he realized we weren't coming back, he waved his gun and shook his fist, got on his camel and rode off. We will find out what happens when we get to Suez.

November 18—We raised the anchor at 09:00 and tried again for Port Suez. The sea was rough but by noon it had calmed down, and we were motor-sailing again.

November 19—We sighted the light off Suez at 05:00 and tied up in Port Suez at 08:30. The log read 1,913 miles. It was a hell of a passage, taking twenty-one days to cover 1,200 miles. A ship's agent came aboard at 09:00. I never wanted an agent before but in this port it paid off. He took care of everything, and by 10:00 we had fuel and water, plus we were cleared to transit the canal the next day. I have never seen anyone work so fast. He also took us into town for provisions. It would have taken me a week to do what the agent did in only a few hours. We came in flying the American flag and passed the *Fairweather* off as an American boat. The canal zone authority even photostatted the British registry and didn't catch the discrepancy. I really worried about that. I had dinner with the Captain of an Egyptian survey ship.

November 20—The pilot came aboard at 12:30 and we started through the canal in a convoy of one. Just before we left, the agent gave me a prayer rug, which was very nice of him, but I haven't been able to find a use for it. We tied to a buoy at El-Kabret at 16:00, and the pilot said he would be back at 07:00 in the morning.

Indian Ocean

November 21—We got underway at 07:00. Our pilot is Greek and speaks English well. He liked to repeat the name and flag of each ship as it passed us. We anchored in front of the sailing club in Ismailla at 13:00. The Commodore rowed out and offered us the use of the club's facilities. After the boys washed the oil from the topsides that we had picked up in Port Suez, we went ashore where we were met with hot showers, cool beer, and excellent food. We met Emile May. After a few bottles of wine, everyone was in high spirits.

November 22—A new pilot came on board at 06:00 and we were on our way again. The new pilot was Egyptian and didn't speak any English or French. And his hand signals were indecipherable. The only thing we could understand was the whirling motion of his hand to indicate *faster*. He seemed rather frustrated and didn't seem to realize that we couldn't go any faster. Halfway to Port Said we came upon a dredger that had a cable across the canal. We were almost on top of it before we saw it. The workers were yelling and waving their arms. We put the boat in reverse but couldn't stop soon enough. Then the workers dropped the chain just in time, as we swung around and just missed the side of the canal with our bowsprit. We arrived in Port Said in the afternoon, dropped the anchor at the sailing club and tied stern-to. We heard that President Kennedy had been assassinated.

Mandraki Harbor

Fairweather *spend six months in Rhodes, Greece, where Mel gave birth to her and Rick's daughter, Tiare. In the photo,* Fairweather *is tied stern-to at the breakwater with her sails drying in Mandraki Harbor. On the left is the market place, and in the far background is the dim outline of the Turkish coast.*

Mediterranean

November 22—We met Emile, Theo, and Catherine and had some home-made rum on board their boat. Afterwards I went to the port officials and didn't have any problem, but then the police came down and dropped off one of their men on *Fairweather*. I said I didn't want a policeman, but they said he had to stay to guard the boat. Another official came down and I told him I didn't want a policeman on board, so they took him off. I had to sign a paper saying I didn't want a policeman. Seems we are the only yacht that has gotten away with not having a "guard" on board.

December 6—Going to a pub or restaurant and ordering a bottle of beer entitles you to all sorts of small dishes: shrimp, olives, pickles, peanuts, and so forth. The first night out Rick, Mel, Ray, and I ate dozens of raw oysters. We were sick for days afterwards. A few nights ago Ray, Verne, Jon, Mel, and Emile went out. As they were walking down the sidewalk after leaving a pub, a young Egyptian spat on Mel. Ray knocked him down and within seconds there was a mob of Egyptians on the street. Jon saw Ray being mobbed, went to help, and began pulling attackers off of Ray. Verne saw Ray and Jon, ran back to help, and was attacked by another mob. The police got there just in time or those three boys might have been killed by that mob. They were taken to the police station, where they signed a statement of the affair, and paid a small fine for disturbing the peace. In the meantime Mel rushed back to the boat very excited, saying the boys were in jail after taking a terrible beating. This was at 01:00. There was nothing I could do at that time, so we waited up and about 03:30 the boys arrived back at the boat. Ray's face was marked up, but they seemed to be in pretty high spirits. They said that the Captain of Police was sympathetic towards them because Jon looked like the actor in the TV series, *Adventures in Paradise*.

Earlier that same night I had gone over to the harbor master's home for a drink. He wanted to meet a woman captain. The outcome of the evening was we are getting the boat hauled out tomorrow for free. We have to furnish our own paint and labor. We have no anti-fouling paint for the bottom but the harbor master seemed to think I could get some off an American freighter, the *Oceanic*, which was in port discharging wheat. The next morning Rick and I took a launch over to her, but the policeman at the top of the gangway wouldn't allow us on board, even with our passes. A few minutes later the Captain came down and invited us aboard. He just told the policemen to let us through. The Captain said he didn't have any anti-fouling paint, but after a few minutes of talking, he invited us up for lunch. That policeman came up and said we had no passes and had to leave, but the Captain told him to go away. At lunch the Captain asked if there was any food we needed. Oh, yes. So they filled four boxes of food for us. Then we had a time getting the food off the ship. That damn policeman wanted us to go to customs with it and pay a fee. The Captain gave him a carton of cigarettes and another one for the man in the launch. We didn't get the paint but we made out alright.

Well, we brought the boat over to the slipway Saturday and as soon as Rick saw it he said we couldn't be hauled out on that thing. It was made for a flat bottom boat—there were no arrangements for the keel. It was obvious they had never hauled a keel boat out before. Even after explaining to them what was wrong with the slipway, they still insisted it was alright, so we backed out and left.

December 10—Ray, Verne, Jon, Sue, Pat, and I went to Cairo with Catherine and Emile. We saw the pyramids, rode the camels, and paid our baksheesh. That night we went to an Egyptian restaurant and then to a night club to see a belly dancer. It was fun being a tourist.

December 13—Port Captain Fawad came over tonight for drinks. We never laughed so much in our lives—what a conceited man, but he was very entertaining with a series of stories about his humble life and his four palaces.

We have no heat on board and it's miserably cold. We had to give up our sandals and buy shoes and winter clothes to keep warm. We've enjoyed Egypt very much: the people, the food, the sights, but there is so much tension in the air because the country is essentially a police state. Everything has been nationalized, so there are no longer any private businesses. The former owners still work at their former companies and are paid a small living allowance. But no one is allowed to make more than $10,000 a year—the rest goes to the government. It's illegal to exchange money anywhere except at a bank, yet there are money changers in town. The legal exchange rate is 43 piasters for a dollar, but

Beirut

Beirut was a beautiful and cosmopolitan city, but the storms in December made getting ashore difficult. Fairweather *was tied stern-to at the seawall, but so far off that the crew used the dinghy to go ashore. When a storm came, the crew had to stand watch in port, in case the stern lines parted and the schooner dragged her anchor.*

money changers give up to 70 piasters. One telling example of the political situation here is that it is impossible to buy charts of the Mediterranean. It seems the government is afraid people will flee the country with money and valuables if they have the chance (the desert takes care of the other borders). This is especially hard on foreigners, like Emile, Theo, and Catherine, who have lived and worked in Egypt for years and have a small yacht. I wired the San Francisco Instrument Company to air mail me charts for the eastern Mediterranean, including a few extra ones that we won't need ourselves.

December 19—We left Port Said for Beirut at 14:30. When I got my clearance today, one of the men at the customs office wouldn't talk to me because I didn't have an agent. Fortunately, a second man had read about us in the newspaper, so he took care of the details. It cost forty piasters for stamps and another sixty for the man to get them. Then I had to go over to the harbor and light section where I was charged another thirty-three piasters. I told the official that I had already paid the light fee, but he said the money wasn't for the fee but for the stamps. Then he asked how many crew members I had, and when I said eight, he replied that that was too many. All other yachts had only three or four crew members. Why did I need eight? I told him they were all my family, and after that the officials were all very courteous.

There was very little wind and what wind we had was dead ahead. We powered all night in calm seas and heavy mist. The engine kept the boat below nice and warm.

December 20—Light winds from the east. We raised sails and were making four to five knots, until the wind died at noon. Now the sea is calm and the engine is on.

December 21—We anchored in Beirut at 14:00. The log read 276 miles. I took a launch ashore and got cleared with no trouble. The man with the launch wanted ten pounds to take me ashore and back—a distance of 100 yards. I told him he was joking and offered him two pounds. He refused. But next day he came back for the two pounds.

Beirut is a cosmopolitan city and—like San Francisco—built on hills. Rate of exchange is three pounds to the dollar. We moved the boat over near the yacht club and tied stern-to at the breakwater, but it's still difficult getting into town.

For Christmas Eve we went aboard a Polish freighter for drinks. They had some strange food to eat but a lot of beer, wine and brandy to drink. What a drunken mob they turned out to be. The wind came up so we had a good excuse to leave. And boy did the wind come up. The waves came crashing over the breakwater and onto the boat. *Fairweather* was rolling wildly—just like being at sea. It was a very miserable night.

Christmas day it was blowing so hard we couldn't get off the boat to go ashore for our Christmas dinner. We had to eat salami sandwiches instead. Three crew members from the Polish freighter came over, but they had to leave after three minutes. *Fairweather* was rolling so much they got seasick.

December 26—Today turned out fair, so we went into town for dinner to make up for the one we missed on Christmas. We heard that there is fighting in Cyprus between the Greeks and the Turks. I hope they get it sorted out before we get there.

January 5, 1964—We left Beirut at 15:00. The situation in Cyprus is still unsettled, so we got clearance today for Rhodes. I think we will like it better there anyway. Cocktail hour has been changed to 12:00 to 13:00, because it's dark and cold at the regular hour of 16:00 to 17:00.

January 9—We arrived in Rhodes at 09:00 and tied stern-to in Mandráki Harbor. An east wind came up on Jon's watch the night before last, so we were able to sail the rest of the way to Rhodes. It started raining last night on Ray's watch and that made it really cold. Jon came off his watch and turned on the stove to warm his hands. Verne came in the galley and wanted to know what that horrible smell was. Jon's hands were so numb he couldn't feel the hair being burnt off them.

It is a remarkable change to be away from the oriental culture and mentality. No guards or gates to pass through when going ashore. Everyone in Rhodes is polite and courteous to each other and to strangers. I think we are going to like it here. Well, we better since we are staying for the next five or six months.

The American Coast Guard is stationed here with Voice of America. They have a school for their children and Sue and Pat are able to attend. The lessons are based on the Calvert Course. The first Saturday here Pat went down to the stadium and played baseball with the American kids. The coach thought it was terrible that an American boy had never played baseball before. That might have helped to get them accepted at the school. A boy at school asked Pat how many languages he could speak and Pat said three:

American, Australian, and English. Gosh, said the boy, you sure are smart. Sue and Pat got their report cards and they passed with above average grades. They seem very happy in school.

The Coast Guard has a private club named after their ship, *Courier*. Drinks and food are cheap. They have made us associate members so we can use the facilities. The Americans are very friendly but rather clannish. Very few of them seem to like the Greeks. They are all looking towards the day when they can go home. I can't understand why. They have a Little America here. All the food is shipped over for them—even clothes.

It won't be long before Mel won't be able to climb on and off the boat. So she and Rick got an apartment up on the hill. Verne and Ray each rented a room there. Verne's room is like an artist's den and Ray's is "Darky's Bar."

Jon and Verne started working for Page Construction, putting up the new Voice of America station south of the town. They started at 50 cents an hour doing rigging work. Two weeks later their wages were raised to sixty-five cents and now they are making one dollar an hour.

We have been here six weeks and still like it. Greeks are fine people as long as you don't do business with them. One of the cylinders on the engine wasn't working so Rick got a diesel mechanic to fix it. He took out all the injectors and checked them. Ok. But when he put them in again he didn't or couldn't time them. We had to have some of our friends on another yacht do it. The Greek charged 600 drachmas for a half-an-hour job. I refused to pay it, so he took the bill to the Port Captain, and then we paid 400 drachmas.

Mediterranean

Rick has gone to Athens to see about having *Fairweather* hauled out. Can't get it done here and if they could they want to charge 200 dollars. Rick returned with Catherine Zarb for a four day visit. We aren't going to Athens now. It's getting close to Mel's time, so we will wait in Rhodes. The weather is too unsettled to leave in any case. We met the Irving Johnsons on their new ketch, *Yankee*. They came into Mandráki Harbor at night during a storm. It's a beautiful center-cockpit boat, built especially for European canal travel. They had heard of the woman skipper.

March 3—Students demonstrated against the Americans here today. There were hundreds of them running through the streets. They threw rocks at the Turkish Consulate, broke the windows at the Voice of America office, and then ran as a mass to the Coast Guard ship *Courier* and threw rocks at it. They also threw rocks at the American school.

March 6—King Paul of Greece died today.

May 1—Mel had a baby girl this morning by caesarian. Both are fine.

Buzz called last month saying Bill left with all the company money, which will probably cause LuRay to go bankrupt. That kind of leaves us here in Rhodes holding an empty sack. I hope he sends us some money so we can get out of here. We need to get the boat hauled, and Mel's hospital bill for sixteen days was 235 dollars.

May 28—Sue graduated into high school with a B average. Pat is now in the seventh grade.

May 30—Sue was riding on the back of a Vespa when they had a spill. She could have broken some bones but only skinned her arm up. We are getting ready to leave

Rhodes. Never heard from Bill, which means we are now on our own financially. The more I think about it the more contemptible his actions seem. Tinned food—what there is to buy—is expensive. Our meals will not be of the best from now on. At least fresh food is cheap. The generator went out the night before we were to sail. Rick and Ray worked half the night repairing it.

June 2—We cleared Rhodes for Symi at 10:00. I still can't believe that we have finally left. We had a head wind all day, but managed to reach Symi before dark and drop the anchor at 18:30. The baby slept all the way. The rolling of the boat seems to agree with her.

June 3—We left Symi for Kos at 05:30. No wind and calm seas. We powered all the way and arrived at 14:30. It was the hottest day I have experienced in seven months, ever since we left Aden. We passed the inner harbor before we saw it. It's nearly circular with a narrow entrance. Kos is as modern as Rhodes without the tourists. Everything was much cheaper in Kos. We paid 32 drachmas for a kilo of meat in Rhodes and in Kos we paid 25 drachmas. The baby was good and we took her ashore and had a beer.

Jon's glands in his neck are swollen and he doesn't feel good. Kos is the island of Hippocrates, the father of medicine—so they should have good doctors here. We located a doctor and were ushered into his presence: the doctor was in bed. One of the questions the doctor asked Jon was if he could "piss good." He gave Jon a prescription for some antibiotics, sure hope they make him better.

June 4—We left Kos at 09:00 and tied up in Kalymnos at 13:00. No wind so we powered all the way. Jon still isn't feeling well, although he says he feels a little better. Rick went shopping for lettuce, and with the head of lettuce he got a spring onion and a green fern, all for one and a half drachmas. People make their living by sponge diving. The Greek boys were a pest. We had a hell of a time keeping them off the boat. Only place in the world we had that kind of problem.

June 5—We left Kalymnos at 06:00 and anchored in Leros at 01:00. We wanted to get there early in the day to do some skin diving. In one of the books I read, it says there are a lot of fish. We anchored in a little cove near the entrance to the harbor. The water was clear and warm but there were no fish. Later, we moved over to the town of Lakki and tied stern-to. The place was empty. It says in the Greek sailing directions that there are facilities to haul out here. It seems to be another misprint or more out-of-date information. It was extremely hot and no one wanted to spend any time here. If we leave this evening, we can make Mykonos by tomorrow evening. I had a little trouble getting my papers because the officer wasn't there to sign them, but when the enlisted sailors saw I was determined to leave, they gave me the papers anyway.

June 5—We left Lakki for Mykonos at 10:00. The wind was blowing fair as we approached Mykonos at 14:00, so we decided to continue on to Syros. We tied up stern-to in Syros at 17:00. We made arrangements to have the boat hauled out on Monday. When Rick first went to the boatyard, the owner wanted $400 just to haul the boat out of the water. Rick told him he was joking. Later that evening he made an offer of $130, so we accepted.

June 9—The boat was hauled yesterday. Today we finished all the painting and are ready to go back in the water

Fairweather

Mel and Tiare

Rick and Mel's daughter, Tiare, was born in Greece and sailed on Fairweather *with the rest of the family back to San Francisco. She quickly learned to get around on the boat, but she couldn't crawl on her hand and knees because the motion of the boat knocked her over. So she sat on her butt and scooted about the cabin floor. On deck she always had a harness on her. She liked the water, and whenever she was near a swimming pool, she scooted over to it and flopped in.*

in the morning. It's a curious twist—the Egyptians wanted to haul us out for free on the same type of slipway, and we turned them down because we thought they didn't know what they were doing, and here in Greece we pay $130 for an even worse slipway. Five gallons of bottom paint cost thirty-three dollars.

June 10—The little guy who put us on the slipway all by himself, put us back in the water all by himself. He worked like a demon all morning and by noon he was ready. While he was working, he kept saying that he was going home to bed—for the last three nights he has been drinking with the boys. When *Fairweather* slid off the slipway, she went into the water with a splash. It was like a new launching. We moved back over to the center of Ermoupoli. A big Greek charter boat came in beside us with a crowd of Americans from L.A. They invited us over for cocktails. We had a good time, very interesting people.

June 11—We left Syros for Kea at 06:00. With the wind from the north, we were able to set the sails. It's raining. What weather. We arrived at Kea and anchored at 15:00. We couldn't tie up to the quay because the northeast wind was blowing too strong.

June 12—We sailed for Vouliagmeni at 06:00 with the wind from the north. We arrived in the rain at 15:00. The marina was full, so we had to anchor in the harbor. We didn't know when we could move into the marina, maybe days or weeks, so we decided to leave for the Zea Marina at Piraeus.

June 13—We powered over to Zea at 08:00 and tied up to the breakwater. Yachtsmen warned us that it's a dirty harbor and they were right. There are a lot of yachts here but most of them are charter boats. The Greeks are enlarging the Zea Marina, and it will be nice when they finish. Right now there is a pile driver pounding piles from 06:00 to 18:00 every day. The vibrations in the water sound like someone is knocking on our keel. Sue and I took the first bus that came by and rode it into Piraeus where we caught the subway to Athens. Sunday Pat and I played tourist and saw the Acropolis.

June 15—Rick and Mel went to the American Consulate to register their daughter, Tiare, as an American citizen. While they were gone, the Navy (Greek) came by and told us to move out of the marina because an Italian destroyer was arriving in the morning. So at 17:00 we powered back to Vouliagmeni. There was one slip free and we raced a Greek kaiki for it, but we lost. We anchored out that night but the next morning we were able to move into a slip in the marina. There are lots of beautiful yachts here but most of them are charter boats. Bill and Gerta on the *New World* are here boat-sitting the *Westward*. There are two sets of showers: one for the crew at three drachmas and one for the captains at six drachmas. There are also separate snack bars. Very nice. The people at the marina are very pleasant. I ordered a bonded case of cigarettes and a case of gin. The good thing about bonded supplies here is that we can use them while still in port.

I went back to the Acropolis with Jon to take some photos. It's a miserable chore getting to Athens and back. The average time takes about seven hours.

June 23—We cleared Vouliagmeni for the Corinth Canal at 06:00. The winds were very unpredictable. At first we had a strong wind and good sailing, then the wind died and it was dead calm. But as soon as we lowered sails, the wind came up again. Everyone told me how the authorities try to charge 600 drachmas for going through the canal, when the charge is supposed to be 177 drachmas. I was all set to argue with the fellow when he came aboard, but it was all for nothing because he only asked for 177 drachmas. The canal is about four miles long and very narrow, with high cliffs on both sides. When we got through the canal, the wind was blowing strong. It looked calmer to the north—to the left of where the town of Corinth is—so we powered over there and tied up in Loutraki at 15:00. The wind blew down from the mountains in big gusts and it was pretty miserable. People on the dock asked the same questions we hear everywhere: How did we get here? Did we *really* sail all the way from America?

June 24—We left Loutraki for Aiyiou at 06:00. Not that Aiyiou was a place of interest, as I've never heard of it before, but it would make a good day's run. There was no wind in the Gulf of Corinth, and so we had to power. We arrived in Aiyiou at 16:30. It was hot. First thing we did was get a cold beer, but only one, since money is short. Ray buys his own. Verne doesn't drink any. Sue said there was an American movie in town, so Ray, Pat, and I went to see it. It turned out to be a German movie with Greek subtitles. We left in the middle of it.

June 25—We left Aiyiou at 08:00 for Patras at the southwestern end of the gulf. There wasn't enough water at the dock to bring *Fairweather* close enough to use a gangplank, so we anchored and went ashore in the dinghy. Patra is a big city. We stayed overnight, then powered over to the island of Ithaka at 05:30. The channel between two high hills opens up into a big bay with the town of Ithaka at the far end. An earthquake destroyed the city in 1953 and it has been completely rebuilt with an Italian flavor. To me Ithaka is the loveliest island we have visited in all of Greece. Odysseus was from here, and we have all been reading about his travels. I hiked up to see the cave where he was supposed to have hidden his boat, but couldn't find it.

June 29—We stayed over the weekend in Ithaka and left this morning at 06:00 for Argostolion on the neighboring island of Kefalonia. Rick bought 125 gallons of diesel in Ithaki at seven drachmas a gallon. We powered all the way and arrived in Argostolion at 14:30. We took on water and we all took a shower while we had the hose.

June 30—We cleared Kefalonia for Reggio di Calabria in Italy at 10:00. Winds were light and made pleasant sailing. We all had a last look at Greece.

July 1—On Verne's watch 12:30 to 15:00 the wind came up from the north and was soon a full gale, with high, short seas. We shortened sail to the storm trysail. While taking in the jib, Rick thought he would drown before the bowsprit came back out of the water. We took on more water during this storm than at any other time. The motion in the main cabin was so unpredictable that the gimbaled table began swinging wildly and then flew apart. The lead weight in the table just missed Jon, who was sleeping in his bunk. Oh man, water was everywhere and everyone was seasick except the baby. Thank goodness she is so good.

Ray said this was a hell of a way to be going to see the Italians. All during his watch he heaved into a bucket that was tied around his neck, and in between heaves, he said he was going to punch the first Italian he saw. Mel was doing pretty well with her own bucket. We've all had some unscheduled salt water showers while on watch. We all seem to be in a bad way. Rick had a pack of cigarettes in his hand, and when Mel handed him a disposable diaper to throw overboard, he threw the cigarettes overboard instead.

In the evening the wind and seas dropped down to nothing. We then powered all night and arrived in Reggio at 12:30. The log read 243 miles. We were flying the American flag and I told the port authorities the boat was American, but those smart guys looked up the port of registry: Georgetown, Grand Cayman, so they knew it was British. Now we are flying the British flag. They were certainly nice about it. No port charges here.

We went out for a real Italian spaghetti dinner. A plate cost 200 lire. I thought we were getting away cheap until the bill came. There was 200 lire for the use of the table cloth, forks and knives, napkins, and 300 lire for service charge. We had three bottle of wine that only cost 600 lire. From now on we'll bring our own table cloth. Enjoyed Reggio but was ready to leave after two days. Everything but the wine was too expensive: meat is $1.50 a pound. The harbor was filthy with oil. Very few people spoke English.

July 5—We left Reggio for Vibo Valentia at 05:30. If more people don't speak English, we'll have to learn another language. There was no wind but there were wild currents in the Straits of Messina. We powered all the way to Vibo Valentia and arrived at 14:30.

July 6—We left Vibo Valentia for Cattraro at 05:40. No wind, so we powered all the way. We arrived in Cattraro and dropped anchor at 15:30. We went swimming over the side, and then Sue cooked spaghetti the way I like it. No one went ashore.

July 7—We left Cattraro for Salerno at 10:00. Still no wind. We powered through the night and tied up in Salerno at 07:30. We found the food cheap, except of course for the meat. It's $1.50 a pound. Rick bought two kilos of small fish for 500 lire. Mel fried them up and they were really good. While in Salerno, we took on water and then started washing down the decks when some character came over and wanted 1500 lire for the water. Rick told him to bring a bill down, so he did. He had added 750 lire for overtime. I told him 1500 lire was too much. He said if I argued, I would have to pay overtime for that too. I told him he must be joking, so he said Ok pay 2,250 lire. I said no. He went and got the Port Captain who said the 1500 lire was correct. Then the Port Captain said Ok, give him five packs of cigarettes for the overtime. I said he was crazy as hell (He couldn't understand me) and then I paid the 1,500 lire and that was that.

July 10—We cleared Salerno for Capri at 10:30, and we finally got some wind: dead ahead from the southwest. It took us eight hours to make the eighteen miles to Capri. The small harbor was so packed that we had to tie up to another boat. Then we found out we couldn't stay there because of the tourist boats that come in during the day and we had to leave at 07:00. We thought it might be calm on the other side of the island, and we would be able to anchor there, but it wasn't, so we went on to Naples. We tied up at the Naples Rowing Yacht Club at 12:30. It's a very nice club.

Mediterranean

I ate something in Capri and when we got to Naples I was really sick. I didn't get out of my bunk for two days. The kids spent their time at the swimming pool here. When I was feeling better, Jon, Pat, and I took the bus to Pompeii. That was the most interesting tourist trip (outside of Africa) that I've been on.

The people here have been so nice we had open house for them. So first we really cleaned the boat up. We got rid of all the boxes and junk on deck that we have carried across two oceans. What a difference it makes. Now the boat no longer looks like Noah's Ark. Sue invited her friends—30 of them. Oh god what a mob. They went through the food like locusts. But what a success our open house turned out to be. It was nothing like the one in Nouméa, where hardly anyone came.

At midnight they invited us over to the club for a real spaghetti meal—the type they eat every evening. It was terrible (at least I thought so). The spaghetti was served with oil, onions, and garlic—there was no tomato sauce. Those Italians ate it like it was delicious. I wouldn't call these Italians crude but maybe exuberant. I met Commander Oliver of the Coast Guard through Metz. He wants to write a story about us but I'm waiting until we get back. He wanted to sail over to Ischia with us so I invited him and his two daughters.

July 29—We left Naples for the Island of Ischia at 10:00, making a beautiful exit and putting on the show for the commander. Set all our sails including the topsail and fisherman. Ray and Verne got in the dinghy and took pictures of *Fairweather*. The wind was light and we had a beautiful sail. By 15:00 we could still see the American Consulate

FAIRWEATHER

Bonifacio

Every time Fairweather *entered a port, the captain had to deal with an array of local officials: harbor master, customs, immigration, police, navy, and in some cases, medical officials. These officials were often the first impression the captain and crew got of a country. Suttie was always polite but insistent with those officials who created difficulties.*

in Naples, so we turned on the engine and powered into Ischia at 20:00. We tied up stern-to and put out our wild gang plank. Ray had painted it the colors of the rainbow. If I had known Ischica was such a beautiful place, we would have come over here sooner, instead of staying in Naples waiting for our mail. For one dollar we can take the ferry to Naples and back.

The clothes in the shops are beautiful and reasonable. I don't know if it's because we have been away from fashion for so long, but these clothes are out of this world. As I remember, a few women were nicely dressed in Beirut. But I haven't seen clothes like this since leaving San Francisco. When I look right and left, I see flags from around the world on the stern of the other yachts in the harbor. Next to us is a French boat with one man on board who doesn't or refuses to speak English. It's wonderful because I must practice my French. Next to him is a German boat. They speak excellent English. Some great parties took place on our boats.

I made arrangements to take on diesel through customs on Saturday. It didn't come but I was told it would be here on Monday, which was fine because we weren't leaving until Tuesday. Monday evening the fellow came by and said the customs here are strict, but we would get our diesel Tuesday for sure. Getting the fuel through customs cost thirty lira; otherwise it cost seventy-five lira. So I said Ok, we will wait another day. Tuesday night he came by and said he couldn't get it but if we went over to Pozzuoli on the mainland, we could pick it up. I asked if he could have the diesel and all the papers ready by 10:00 because I would be there then. Oh yes! he said. We were in Pozzuoli

Ajaccio

The crew worked on the boat in the morning and had the afternoon free. In port, the main meal of the day was dinner at 13:00. Money was becoming tight, but still the food was plentiful if somewhat bland. The only luxury was the afternoon beer. In the photo, Rick and Ray are sitting at an open cafe in Ajaccio, Corsica.

at 10:00 but we didn't get our diesel until 18:00. I was fuming at the Italians. If we didn't need the fuel I would have taken off just as the fuel truck arrived. And on top of that he had added an extra 5000 lira to the bill, which he said was for the customs. Ha—I refused to pay it. I had the fuel and paid him only what he quoted me. Soon as he got off the boat we left for the Island of Ponza.

We powered all night and anchored in Ponza at 07:30. We stayed at anchor in the clear water and spent two days diving to clean the bottom of the boat. There was so much growth on the bottom that we had been making only three knots under power. I never went into town. I like the Italians, but some of them are impossible.

August 7—We left Ponza for Corsica, France, at 17:30. We sailed off the anchor and the current helped carry us out of the harbor, and we drifted slowly all night. In the morning the wind came up and we were able to average four knots all day. Then the wind began to increase and by the next morning, we were hove-to. We couldn't raise a sail until the following day. The wind was from the west, dead ahead. We could head north toward Elba or south toward Sardinia, so we headed north. In the evening the wind shifted to the southwest and we headed more to the west. By morning the wind dropped and we powered to Porto Vecchio on the east coast of Corsica and tied up next to a lot of other yachts. There was no bank in town, so I couldn't get any money exchanged. An American yacht helped out and then we were able to get a cool beer at a little stand on the beach.

I hiked into town later in the evening, which was quite a walk uphill. The town is very touristy. There are a lot of

French people here on vacation, either on their small boats or camping out in tents. We cleared for all France—no one at the Port Authority spoke any English. Nobody speaks English. We stayed till Thursday morning then set sail for Bonifacio. We had a good sail, the best since arriving in the Mediterranean. Bonifacio has a long narrow harbor, with high hills on both sides. The wind was blowing out of the harbor as we tacked in and tied up at 17:00.

There is no bank here either. There were a lot of yachts arriving and departing. We are flying the American flag again. Ray and Rick went spear fishing and brought back some beautiful fish that looked something like trout. They were cleaning them on the pier when a fellow without a shirt came over and told them (in French) to be sure to clean off the pier when they were done. Then the fellow went away and came back a few minutes later in a uniform and wanted to know if we had a fishing permit. We said we couldn't understand his French. He got very excited and kept demanding to see our permit, and then he said we shouldn't be tied up at this quay. We said we didn't understand him. He spent an hour trying to find someone who could speak English, but everyone seemed to know that he was some sort of bastard and so he couldn't find anyone to interpret for him. We may have spoilt his day, but he spoilt our stay in Bonifacio.

August 16—We sailed for Propriano at 06:00. The wind was from the northwest and we spent all day trying to get past the light on Les Moines. Propriano was only seventeen miles but we couldn't make it before dark, so we continued on under sail for Ajaccio, the capital of Corsica.

Mediterranean

August 17—We arrived in Ajaccio at 08:30. I like this place the best of all Corsica. There are a lot of yachts tied up at the quay where there is water for showers and general cleaning. And the town is at the harbor, so shopping is convenient. There is a lot of good food for sale, but meat is still out of our price range. I would like to spend a week here but we must move on.

August 19—We left Ajaccio for Baie de Sagone at 06:30. We picked up only one other anchor as we pulled away from the quay. That was lucky—the day before we watched as boat after boat fouled its anchor while leaving. The wind was from the northwest and blowing strong, plus there were huge, uncomfortable seas, but we are making seven knots. At noon the wind dropped but there were still high seas. One sea knocked us on our beam. The sails took a beating with the motion and then the main ripped, making an awful sound. We took down the main and powered into anchor at Baie de Sagone, where we spent the afternoon sewing the mainsail. We set sail again for Calvi at 19:30.

The wind shifted to the southwest and by 22:00 it was blowing a full gale. We were lucky we weren't caught in Baie de Sagone, which is fully exposed to the southwest. We average seven knots with the wind and high seas. Then as we rounded Revellata Point to Calvi, the dinghy, which we were pulling astern, broke lose. I dreamt last night that we lost the dinghy at night. Lucky it happened during the daylight. The wind was howling as we came about for the dinghy. We anchored in Calvi harbor at 08:30 and slept nearly all day. The harbor was full of boats waiting out the storm.

Fairweather

San Tropez

In San Tropez, as in a number of Mediterranean ports, Fairweather *was tied up next to large luxury yachts, the kind that have uniformed crews. So tourists, and even locals, looked at* Fairweather *as something of an oddity, with her old-fashioned wooden hull and cotton sails, and what must have looked to them like a tangled mass of rigging. For some reason, people stopped and asked the same questions over and over: "Do you anchor at night?" And referring to the baggywrinkle, "What is that fuzzy stuff in the rigging?"*

Mediterranean

August 21—We sailed for Monaco the next day at 11:00. The wind was from the northeast, making our course a perfect beam reach. So instead of arriving in Monaco at 12:00, as we had expected, we arrived at 03:00 and hove-to until daylight. We planned to stay only one day to pick up our mail, but Monaco was such a beautiful place that we stayed four days, and we would have stayed even longer, but we had to move on. The first night in Monaco Verne, Ray, Rick, Mel, and I went to the Casino. We asked the people on the next boat what it was like and what we should wear. They said black tie, of course. Well, we didn't have any clothes like that, so we put on our best and went. We were as well dressed as anyone else there.

On our second day in Monaco, Sue decided to take Mario, the parrot that we've had since Mazatlán, for a walk. We were tied stern-to, and as Sue walked down the gangplank with Mario on her shoulder—where he had spent many hours—he flew off. Sue hadn't clipped his wings in a while and they had grown out enough for him to fly up the hill and disappear. Sue and Pat searched for him all day but it was adios Mario.

August 25—We sailed from Monaco at 10:00 and arrived in Nice at 13:00. The four days in Monaco cost twenty francs to tie up at the quay. There was no place to tie up in Nice, except at the commercial dock, so we decided to leave in the morning for Cannes. As we cleared the harbor, we saw the Dutch boat we met in Monaco sailing for Cannes, so we powered over to her and raised our sails to race them. There wasn't enough wind for us and they beat us badly. There was one good slip left in Cannes when we arrived at 13:00. The harbor is very crowded and many of the boats are tied up three abreast.

August 31—We left Cannes for Saint Tropez at 09:00. The winds were light from the south, and we arrived in Saint Tropez at 14:00. We tied stern-to at the quay, squeezed between two large power yachts, the kind of yachts that have uniformed crews. The quay seemed to be the main street of the town. We were sitting in the stern, drinking gin during our cocktail hour and watching the crowd walk by, when a couple stopped to look at *Fairweather*. The man turned to the woman and said, "this is a real yacht, not like all these gin palaces here."

September 2—We sailed from Saint Tropez at 07:00. The wind was moderate from the east, and we dropped anchor off Isle du Levant at 16:00. Isle du Levant is a nudist colony, and as soon as the anchor was set, Ray dropped his shorts and dove into the water and started swimming for shore. Pat was right behind him with Verne soon following. The people look like strange animals on the beach. I don't know what it was all about, but for me it was too damn cold. The boys came back for lunch, and afterwards Mel and Sue went ashore. They brought bottoms but no tops, as the boys said all the girls were bare breasted. They felt pretty silly when they found that all the women were fully dressed in town. We raised the anchor at 16:00 and sailed for Porquerallo Isle, where we arrived at 18:00. It was so crowded we had to tie up next to the ferry berth. The bow of one ferry just missed us, so we thought it better to leave in the morning for Toulon.

September 3—We arrived in Toulon at 11:00. We tried to tie up to the quay where all the yachts were, but with the wind blowing so hard, the anchor wouldn't hold. We tried to set it four times but we dragged it all over the bay before it finally held. On the pier was a sign saying this was where all visiting yachts tie up. I loved Toulon because it's not touristy and the people are friendly. We spent four days there.

September 8—We left Toulon for Barcelona at 09:30. We set the sails in a light wind from the south-southwest. We sighted the lights of Barcelona and hove-to off the breakwater at 03:00. The next morning we tied up in Barcelona at the Real Club Nautico. Barcelona is a big city and it's fascinating to walk around and be among so many people. Rick does most of the shopping now, and he is very good at it. I asked him how he gets meat so cheap, and he said that when he gets to the market, he goes downstairs where they sell horse meat. Well, so far no one has said anything about how the meat tastes. Jon and Verne went to the bullfights, and they said there was a big crowd and that one matador even got an ear and a tail for his efforts. They seemed to think that was exciting.

September 23—We left Barcelona for Tarragona at 18:00. There was no wind, so we powered all the way and arrived the next day at 08:00. We had the boat hauled out in Tarragona, and the boys scraped and painted the bottom. I hope the anti-fouling paint is better this time than the one we used in Syros. We had one plank replaced, which cost one-hundred dollars. With only four-hundred dollars a month, I have to buy food for the crew, fuel for the boat, and cover repairs and harbor fees. Everything seems expensive, and everything is stretched thin, especially the food.

October 3—We left Tarragona for Palma at 11:00. Again there was no wind, so we powered all the way and arrived in Palma the following day. We tied up at the Club Nautico at 13:00.

October 9—We left Palma for Ibiza Island at 11:00. The wind was from west and we were on the starboard tack, heading mostly south. The wind continued to make up stronger during the day and evening. At midnight we went on the port tack. The boat was laboring into the seas and we were taking on too much water. The baby is seasick for the first time. We weren't making any headway, so we headed back to Palma and anchored at 11:00 the next morning. This was the first time we ever had to return to a port because of the weather.

October 16—We left Palma for Gibraltar at 12:00. The first day out, we were running before light winds from the north-northeast. Pat started to learn how to use the sextant and work out a sun sight. A few days later the wind died, so we turned on the engine and powered to Malaga.

October 21—We arrived in Malaga at 07:00. We met Dick and Jenny Russell, who we had last seen in Rhodes. We bought 55 gallons of fuel at 6.5 pesetas a gallon, which was enough to get us to Gibraltar. The swell in the harbor was ramming the boat against the pier, so we left Malaga for Gibraltar as soon as the fuel was aboard.

October 23—The wind and seas from the west were strong. In the morning we were on the starboard tack under storm trysail and staysail. In the evening we tacked to port, but we were making no headway, so we returned to Malaga. We were at sea for forty-eight hours and our course on the chart looks like a figure eight. The winds in

Mediterranean

the Mediterranean were very unpredictable and were often too light or too strong to sail in.

October 26—We left Malaga for Gibraltar at 18:00. There was no wind, so we powered all night and arrived in Gibraltar the next morning at 07:00. I bought stores in preparation for crossing the Atlantic, and I was limited mainly to basics: rice, beans, pasta, and flour. No jam this time, but I got a deal on twelve dozen eggs. We dipped them in boiling water for thirty seconds. They'll last that way for weeks. I also bought a new nautical almanac for the next year, 1965. At the end of the shopping, I had fifty cents left and a choice between a kilo of oranges and two bottles of (very cheap) champagne. I bought the champagne.

The Topsail

The crew hoped to make a quick passage of two weeks across the Atlantic, but the winds were light and arbitrary. The trade winds never appeared until within a few days of Barbados. So the crew worked at getting every extra half-knot out of the schooner, which meant setting the topsail. The topsail was a beast. Someone had to go aloft to set it and it often fouled. In the photo, Verne is aloft clearing the topsail sheet and setting the sail on the starboard tack.

Atlantic Ocean

November 16—We left Gibraltar for the Canary Islands at 16:00. The winds were light and from the east. Mel was doing all the cooking, and Ray was learning to navigate. I looked at Ray's plotting sheet and told him that *Fairweather* can't sail on land. We've been learning to take moon sights, and our plotting sheets look like the work of a mad man.

November 24—We sighted the light on Isla de Alegranza at 01:00 and anchored in Las Palmas, Gran Canaria, at 08:00. It was an easy passage. The log read 575 miles.

December 1—We decided to sail to the Cape Verde Islands before crossing the Atlantic. By heading further south before crossing the Atlantic, we hope to catch the trade winds sooner. There are nineteen yachts in Las Palmas getting ready to cross the Atlantic. *Fairweather* and the *Jolly Swagman* are the only yachts that have already made an ocean passage. We first met Brian and Jan on the *Jolly Swagman* in Singapore. They sailed around the Cape of Good Hope, instead of up the Red Sea. They told us that the *Diana*, with Captain Johnson and crew, was lost in a storm off the Cape of Good Hope. Only *Diana's* hatch cover and life ring were ever found.

December 2—We left Las Palmas for the Cape Verde Islands at 16:00. Mel is still having trouble with port and starboard, so we have been calling the port and starboard tacks Mel's and Sue's tacks because their bunks are on the port and starboard sides.

December 4—We are under mainsail and jib, with winds from the east-northeast. We caught a mahi-mahi today and Verne made possion cru.

December 9—We sighted the light on St. Antao at 18:00 and hove-to off St. Vicente all night. When we entered Porto Grande this morning, a pilot boat met us and the pilot came aboard and took over the helm. He was a tall, dark Portuguese-African who spoke perfect English. After we anchored, ten other officials came aboard. Everyone was very pleasant. The log read 815 miles.

Ray, Verne, and I went into Mindelo. Its population is about 30,000, and we saw five white people: Ray, Verne, me, and two others. These are the poorest people I've ever seen. They are dressed in rags and are barefoot. The market place was filthy, and we stuck out like sore thumbs. Later in the day, four islanders rowed out to *Fairweather* to do some trading. We traded a shirt for a boat carved from a horn. After that we traded our old clothes for food. We got eggs, bananas, cooking oil, seven lobsters, three live chickens and three jugs of wine. We cleaned out our clothes. Rick was able to get rid of the grey shoes that he bought in Egypt and that Emile got such a big laugh out of. He got a jug of wine for them.

I went to clear this morning and make arrangements to pick up water. There were no port charges. We brought *Fairweather* up to the water boat in the morning. All the

Atlantic Ocean

water is brought to the island by boat from St. Antao, the next island. The wind has been blowing hard ever since we came in. It blew so hard the first night that it flipped the dinghy over. It has calmed down considerably today, but it is still blowing strong, just not gale force. One of the chickens we got turned out to be a rooster and it started crowing this morning at 03:30. I don't think it will last until Christmas.

December 12—We left Porto Grande for Barbados at 11:00. As soon as we were out of the harbor, the engine started acting up, so we were again without an engine. To reach Barbados before Christmas, we need to make 162 miles a day—an average of six and three-quarters knots. We set the light weather sails: both topsail and fisherman. The wind is from the southeast, and we are supposed to be in the northeast trades.

December 13—We are twenty-four hours out of Porto Grande and we've made only 141 miles. We are losing too much time tacking. Without the engine's help coming into the wind, it sometimes takes us an hour to come about in a heavy sea.

December 14—We are not averaging 160 miles a day. Verne has figured out a series of possible dates for arriving in Barbados. For example, if we average 150 miles a day, we will there by December 26, and if we average 100 miles a day, we will be there by New Years. It is discouraging, especially Verne's last calculation: if we average 17 miles a day, we will be there by Easter.

December 16—I had an accident today. While changing tacks, I ran to grab the jib sheet, tripped and hit my head on the yardarm that's been lashed on deck since Nicobar.

Fishing

Since Fairweather *had no refrigeration, fresh fish was always a welcomed addition to the crew's diet, so the schooner carried a tackle box with fishing gear for making lures: hooks, feathers, swivels, heads, spinners, sinkers, and stainless steel wire. The crew found that a lure with red eyes and yellow feathers worked best, or was just plain lucky. In the photo, Ray holds up a mahi-mahi, as Rick, sitting on the taffrail behind the main sheet, looks on.*

Atlantic Ocean

I broke my left eye tooth off at the gum. It's just hanging there, I don't know by what, but it hurts like hell.

December 18—We're not even averaging a 100 miles a day. Winds are from the south, southwest, west, and northwest. Yesterday there was no wind. Where are the trade winds?

December 19—Light winds from various directions. Verne used a sail cover to rig a bathtub at the foremast.

December 21—Noon. Becalmed with scattered rain. Lowered the fisherman and topsail. The log reads 965 miles.

Lat. 13° 34" N
Long. 41° 55" W

December 23—The wind is from the northwest, shifting to the north. There is a huge swell. Where are the trade winds! The chickens got their sea legs the first day out of Porto Grande. We've been scattering rice on deck for them, and that seems to keep them happy, but they are still as skinny as when we got them. They won't make much of a Christmas dinner.

December 25—It's very calm and very hot.

Lat. 13° 30" N
Long. 46° 57" W

The log reads 1,276 miles, and we are 750 miles from Barbados. For Christmas dinner, Mel cooked fried chicken, mashed potatoes with giblet gravy, fresh squash, cranberry

Valerie Queen

The Valerie Queen *left San Francisco a few days after* Fairweather, *and they met in Cabo San Lucas and Mazatlán. But like numerous other cruising yachts, the* Valerie Queen *was plagued with crew problems, and at one time, Don Stewart even tried to sail the 68-foot schooner alone. He got as far as Bonaire in the Dutch Antilles, where the* Valerie Queen *sank.* Fairweather *stopped in Bonaire and, while diving, the crew saw the wreck on the bottom of the bay.*

Atlantic Ocean

sauce, bread, and fruit cake. After two weeks at sea, it was very good.

December 26—Squalls in the morning. Hot at noon. Very little wind.

December 27—Becalmed. We caught a shark and had it for lunch and dinner. But while letting out the fish line again, it fouled the log line.

December 30—A strong wind from the north, bringing squalls with it.

January 1, 1965—Wind from northeast. Sighted the Barbados light at 18:00.

January 2—We sailed around the southern end of Barbados and anchored in front of the yacht club in Bridgetown at 10:00. The log read 1886 miles. We were twenty-one days at sea. The *Jolly Swagman* is here. She sailed straight from the Canary Islands.

January 6—We had a tug tow us into the careenage and sent to Trinidad for engine parts. Two things that Barbados is known for are flying fish and Mount Gay rum. I prefer the rum and bought a case of it at fifty cents a bottle.

February 1—We've waited three weeks for the engine parts from Trinidad. They never came. We got parts from an American naval repair ship that anchored in the bay for a few days.

February 11—We finally got the engine repaired. It took five weeks and $187. I decided to visit a few islands before heading for Panama, so we left Barbados at 13:00 and set sail for St. Lucia, and arrived the next morning and anchored in Port Castries at 07:30. The boys went into town and bought a block of ice, so with rum, lime, and ice, we had cocktail hour in port.

February 14—We left St. Lucia at 08:00 and sailed for Martinique, and arrived the next afternoon and anchored in Baie de Fort-de-France at 15:00. Jon and Verne made some pocket money sewing sails for another yacht anchored in the bay. Rick bought six loaves of French bread, but most everything else is expensive here, especially since many items are imported from France.

February 17—We left Martinique at 13:00 and sailed for Bonaire in the Dutch Antilles. The wind was light from the southeast. We caught a mahi-mahi and Mel baked bread and made possion cru for dinner.

February 20—We sighted Bonaire before sundown and hove-to for the night.

February 21—We tied to a buoy in front of the Flamingo Hotel at 08:00. The log read 460 miles. We were only a hundred yards from where the *Valerie Queen* sat on the bottom of the bay. The story of Don Stewart is a sad one. He eventually lost his crew and ended up here in Bonaire. One day, while he was ashore, someone yelled that the *Valerie Queen* was sinking at anchor. Don rushed out to the schooner and just managed to run her onto the beach before she sank. The next day, Bonaire customs officials came down and told Don he had to pay an import tax for beaching his boat on the island. Don didn't have the money to cover the tax, so he kedged the schooner off the beach and let her sink in the bay. Now Don is the manager of the Flamingo Hotel.

February 25—Bonaire is a low island and the trade winds blow across it, leaving a layer of fine sand on deck every morning. In fact, there was sand in everything, in our clothes and food, so we were eager to move on. We left

Atlantic Ocean

Bonaire at 10:00 and sailed for Panama. There was a strong wind and high seas from east-northeast.

February 28—Noon: the log reads 609 miles. With a strong wind on our starboard quarter and a heavy following sea, we made 236 miles in the last 24 hours, averaging just under ten knots. It was our best noon-to-noon run.

March 2—We passed through the breakwater in Cristóbal at 09:30. After clearing, we moved over to the yacht club. I met John Dorsa at the yacht club bar. He was our pilot when we made our first canal transit in 1960. And he was very surprised to see us again and not quite as skeptical about our cruise as he was last time we were here.

March 8—We started through the canal at 06:30. There was a strong wind on our stern, making it difficult to control *Fairweather* in the locks. We had a very scary time at first, but later, powering though Gatun Lake and the Gaillard Cut, we were able to relax for most of the day. Now I'm happy to be at anchor in Balboa on the Pacific side.

March 9—We left Balboa and set sail for Acapulco at 19:00. The wind is from the south. For the passage up the coast, we took on extra fuel, four fifty-five gallon barrels lashed to the main shrouds. We are on our way home now and getting to San Francisco is what seems to keep us going.

March 10—We are under sail, with the wind from the northwest. We left Cape Mala astern at the end of my watch.

March 11—We are under power, following the coast and trying to stay under the gales that blow out of the mountains of Central America.

Suttie and Rick

Suttie and Rick, captain and navigator, sitting at the helm. They often spent time together at the helm, as Suttie took over the watch from Rick. They are wearing heavy coats because it was cold heading north off the California coast.

Atlantic Ocean

March 12—Under sail on the starboard tack, with the wind from the west. We caught a mahi-mahi on Ray's watch and had fried fish for lunch and dinner.

March 13—Under power and very hot. Jon saw a turtle, told Rick to come back for him, and jumped in the sea. We threw him a line and he got it around the turtle's flipper so the boys could haul it aboard. Verne butchered it, Mel fried it, and we had turtle steaks for dinner.

March 14—Under sail, crossing the Gulf of Papagayo with the wind from the north.

March 15—A Papagayo hit us in the night. The sudden gale force winds coming out of the mountains ripped the foot of the foresail to shreds. The boys cut up a sail cover and managed to sew it back together.

March 16—Under sail, with the wind from the south. The baby is all over the boat below decks. She can't crawl on her hands and knees because the motion of the boat knocks her over. So she sits on her butt and scoots about the cabin floor at an amazing speed.

March 18—Under sail, with the wind from the west. We are following coast and entering the Gulf of Tehuantepec.

March 20—A Tehuantepec hit us, and we hove-to in gale force winds. In eighteen hours we have drifted forty miles to the south-southwest, at the average of about two knots. The seas are huge, with some breaking on deck. At the height of the gale, Jon caught a mahi-mahi that was swimming under the stern. It was so big he called for Ray and Verne to help him lift it on board.

March 22—The wind dropped enough to set the staysail. Motor sailing, with staysail and trysail. We can see land forward of the starboard beam, but there hasn't been any sun, so we haven't been able to fix our position.

March 24—Motor sailing, with the wind from the west-northwest.

March 25—We entered Acapulco Bay at night—against our better judgment—and anchored at 01:00. But the bay at Acapulco is large and easy to navigate, and we have been here before. The log read 1,421 miles. The boys discovered what was happening to the engine. The heat exchanger was broken and water was backing up into the cylinders. They took it apart to have it welded. As soon as it's repaired and we take on water and fuel, we will continue north. The workers at the yacht club put on a festival, The Day of the Mariner, and invited us to join them. They had a dozen or more sea turtles tied to the yacht club pier. They took them and made a turtle stew and served it with tortillas and beer. It was simple but very good.

April 1—We set sail for Manzanillo at 09:30, with 400 gallons of fuel.

April 4—There has been little wind for the past three days. Motor sailed the whole time.

April 5—We entered Manzanillo Bay at night—another large bay we've been in before—and anchored at 04:00. The log read 342 miles.

April 7—We rested for a day, and last night the boys went ashore to a bar where a plate of boiled shrimp came with each bottle of beer. Mel wanted to go too but the boys said women didn't go there. The bar was pretty dirty and didn't even have a toilet, for men or women. This didn't stop Mel and she went with them. In the morning we took on fuel and water, and then set sail for Cabo San Lucas.

Atlantic Ocean

April 11—No wind for four days. Under power.

April 12—We entered San Lucas Bay at 15:00 and set two anchors, bow and stern. There are no other cruising boats in the bay.

April 15—We took on 200 gallons of fuel and set sail for Turtle Bay.

April 16—We are making little progress with strong winds from the northwest. Noon-to-noon log read 32 miles. It's turning cold.

April 19—It's been calm the last three days. Under power.

April 20—We anchored in Turtle Bay at 15:00. The log read 457 miles. The crew needs a rest.

April 24—After a few days in Turtle Bay, Rick and Verne waved a fishing boat over to *Fairweather* to trade a bottle of rum for some abalone. It was very cheap white rum and no one on board wanted to drink it. Rick thought he could get three or four abalone for it, but the fisherman filled up an entire bucket with abalone that were already shelled. I never thought we would get tired of abalone but we did. This morning, after everyone was well rested, we set sail for San Diego.

April 26—Under power yesterday and today.

April 27—We passed Point Loma at 15:00 and tied up at the San Diego customs dock. The customs officials never came down to the boat. We went to the supermarket and bought food that we hadn't seen in months. The food was too rich and some of us got a little sick from it. I don't think we'll be eating much mayonnaise for a while.

May 2—We took on fuel and water and set sail for San Francisco at noon.

May 7—We've had strong winds from the northwest. Our progress is slow and the nights are very cold. The watch wears a heavy survival suit with lined boots to keep warm.

May 8—We sighted the light ship off Farallon Islands at 05:00 and passed under the Gold Gate in a light fog at 09:00. On one hand it's a relief, but on the other, it's a strange feeling: this is our last port.

The Golden Gate

Fairweather *had light winds and fog, as she approached the Golden Gate, completing her world cruise.*

Afterword

After returning to San Francisco, they often thought that if the world were larger, or perhaps flat instead of round, they would still be on *Fairweather*, sailing further and further to the west. So in a very literal sense, the cruise of the *Fairweather* came to an end because the world is not only round but also 21,600 nautical miles in circumference. In completing that circumference, the compulsion that drove them to continue, especially since Panama, suddenly disappeared. It wasn't that they felt they were home, because they didn't feel that at all, but because they felt they had finished something. They were done, and any further sailing would have nothing to do with the cruise of the *Fairweather*. And there was no motivation, or resources, to slip the mooring lines and take up a new venture.

The first shock that followed the end of the cruise, a shock more dramatic even than the selling of *Fairweather*, was the break up of the crew. Within days of mooring in Sausalito, they became strangers to each other. Once the daily routine on board was abandoned, the ties that had bound them together so tightly for over four years were suddenly gone, and without *Fairweather* as the center of their world, they no longer had anything in common. It was an odd feeling, and for some of them it was an unexpected loss. In four years they had gained a certain sense of the world, but in the end they lost the world of the schooner, the world that made that wider sense of the world possible.

The next shock that followed was that the people they met in San Francisco—some of them friends, and even relatives—had strange, even incomprehensible needs and desires. Only later did they realize that this lack of comprehension was the result of their own lack of imagination. The sea does that to you. The sea is so demanding in the practicalities of life that the imagination is simply lost in the preoccupation with the immediate, with lee shores and gale force winds. In addition, the sea produced in them a certain naive arrogance that they didn't recognize in themselves, an arrogance that derived from their having experienced so much and having learned so little. Again, the sea does that to you.

Even that is now gone and all that remains to them is a few minor idiosyncrasies. Such as a certain insistence on punctuality, as if their lives were still ruled by the ship's clock and it was a matter of honor to relieve the watch on time. And a certain nervousness when the wind blows up and there's nothing to be done, no sails to reef, no lines to coil, and no exhaustion to sleep off. And finally, a desire to live near the sea where they can look to the west and remember what lies beyond the horizon.

www.ingramcontent.com/pod-product-compliance
Lightning Source LLC
Chambersburg PA
CBHW042042290426
44109CB00001B/6